THE POCKET GUIDE TO SEO FOR AUTHORS

THE POCKET GUIDE SERIES #2

TROY LAMBERT

DISCLAMER

Although the publisher and the author have made every effort to ensure that the information in this book was correct at press time, and while this publication is designed to provide accurate information in regard to the subject matter covered, the publisher and the author assume no responsibility for errors, inaccuracies, omissions, or any other inconsistencies herein and hereby disclaim any liability to any party for any loss, damage, or disruption caused by errors or omissions, whether such errors or omissions result from negligence, accident, or any other cause.

The publisher and the author make no guarantees concerning the level of success you may experience by following the advice and strategies contained in this book, and you accept the risk that results will differ for each individual. The testimonials and examples provided in this book show exceptional results, which may not apply to the average reader, and are not intended to represent or guarantee that you will achieve the same or similar results.

FOREWORD

This book is intended to provide you as an author with the basics of SEO best practices in a field that is already rapidly changing. The advent and increased use of generative AI will have an impact on the search industry.

But I believe that certain abiding principles will remain the same. Keywords and content will always matter to search engines. As long as advertising drives search engines, your content and keywords will make a difference in how and when your results show up in search.

No matter what else changes, these will stay the same. So while tools and tips mentioned may age (and if they do, this text will be updated) the essentials of

ONE
AN INTRODUCTION TO SEO

Before we get started, there are some terms we should define and some concepts we should explore. Here are some simple definitions and introductions to SEO and what it means. While this may seem basic, I encourage you to skim this section at least, as it sets the foundation for the rest of this book.

WHAT IS A SEARCH ENGINE?

A search engine is a software program that searches a database of Internet sites, such as Google, Bing, and Yahoo, for keywords and returns a list of the Websites most relevant to the search. The search engine uses algorithms to determine the relevance of the search results based on the words or phrases entered into the search box. The search engine also ranks the results based on their popularity and relevance so that the most valuable and relevant sites are displayed at the top of the list.

A search engine can also be a searchable index of a specific website or online retailer. So your website can have a search engine, just like Amazon and other online retailers do.

HOW DOES IT WORK?

A search engine uses a web crawler, also known as a spider, to scan the Internet and index websites. The search engine maintains a database of all the websites it has discovered and stores the information in its index. When a user searches for something using a search engine, the search engine looks through its index and returns a list of websites relevant to the search query. The search engine also uses algorithms to rank the results, with the most relevant and popular websites appearing at the top of the list.

Here is a brief overview of the process:

1. The user enters a search query into the search engine, using keywords or phrases to describe what they are looking for
2. The search engine searches its index for websites containing the keywords or phrases the user has entered.
3. The search engine ranks the results based on relevance and popularity and displays the most relevant and popular websites at the top of the list.
4. The user can then browse the search results list to find the information they are looking for.

This is a very simplified explanation of how a search engine works. In reality, the process is much more complex and involves many different algorithms and techniques to ensure that the search results are accurate and relevant.

WHAT IS AN ALGORITHM?

An algorithm is a set of steps or instructions followed in a specific order to solve a problem or accomplish a task. Algorithms can be simple, such as a recipe for making a cake, or complex, such as the algorithms used by search engines to rank search results.

Algorithms are an essential part of computer science, and they are used in many different areas, such as artificial intelligence, data mining, and machine learning. They are also used in everyday life, such as GPS systems and financial software.

Algorithms are typically designed to be efficient, meaning they use minimal resources, such as time and memory, to solve a problem. They are also intended to be correct, producing the correct output for a given input.

HOW DO WE TRAIN ONE?

A user can do several things to help improve the chances that their website will be found by a search engine and ranked higher in the search results. Here are a few tips:

1. Create relevant and high-quality content: The content on your website should be relevant to the keywords you are targeting and of high quality. This will help the search engine understand what your website is about and rank it more highly for relevant searches.
2. Use relevant and descriptive titles and tags: The title and tags on your website should be descriptive and include relevant keywords. This will help the search engine understand your website and rank it more highly for relevant searches.
3. Create alt tags to describe all of your images: Alt tags describe the content of images on your website. By including relevant keywords in the alt tags, you can help the search engine understand what your website is about and rank it more highly for relevant searches.
4. Use header tags: Header tags indicate the hierarchy of the content on your website. By using header tags

appropriately, you can help the search engine understand the structure of your content and rank it more highly for relevant searches.

5. Use a sitemap: A sitemap is a file that lists all the pages on your website. By submitting a sitemap to the search engine, you can help the search engine discover and index all the pages on your website more quickly.
6. Use backlinks: Backlinks are links from other websites that point to your website. Having a high number of high-quality backlinks can help improve your search engine ranking.
7. Use social media: By using social media to promote your website and share your content, you can help increase the visibility of your website and improve your search engine ranking.

These are a few simple ways to train an algorithm, and we will explore each in more detail throughout this text.

WHAT IS SEO?

SEO stands for "search engine optimization." It is the practice of optimizing a website to improve its visibility and ranking in search engine results pages (SERPs). When someone searches for a specific term or phrase, search engines like Google use algorithms to determine which websites are the most relevant and authoritative for that search query, and they display those websites at the top of the search results.

WHY IS SEO IMPORTANT FOR AUTHORS?

As an author, having a robust online presence is crucial for reaching potential readers and promoting your books. SEO can help you achieve this by making it easier for people to find your website when searching for keywords related to your books or topics you write about. By optimizing your website for relevant keywords, you can increase your visibility in search results and drive more traffic to your site. This can help you reach a wider audience and sell more books.

In addition, SEO can also help establish your website as an authority on a particular subject or topic. This can increase credibility and trust with readers and potential partners, such as book publishers or agents.

Website authority refers to a website's perceived credibility and trustworthiness in the eyes of both users and search engines. Several types of website authority can impact a website's rankings and visibility in search results.

1. **Domain authority:** This is a measure of a domain's overall credibility and strength based on factors such as the age of the domain, the number and quality of links pointing to the domain, and the presence of a clear hierarchy of pages. Domain authority is often used to predict how well a website will rank in search results.
2. **Page authority:** Like domain authority, page authority is a measure of the credibility and strength of a specific web page. It is based on factors such as the number and quality of links pointing to the page, the relevance of the page's content to the search query, and the presence of structured data.
3. **Trustworthiness** refers to users' perceived level of trust in a website. A website perceived as trustworthy is more likely to be seen as an authoritative source of information and may rank higher in search results.
4. **Expertise:** A website that is perceived as an expert in a particular subject or topic is likely to be seen as more authoritative than a website that is less knowledgeable about the topic. This type of authority can be built by consistently providing high-quality, in-depth content

demonstrating a deep understanding of the subject matter.

The Google E.A.T. principle stands for "expertise, authority, and trustworthiness." It is a set of guidelines that Google uses to evaluate the credibility and quality of websites. According to Google, websites that demonstrate expertise, authority, and trustworthiness in their content and user interactions are more likely to rank highly in search results.

- Expertise refers to the depth of knowledge and understanding a website has about a particular subject or topic. A website perceived as an expert in a specific subject is more likely to be seen as an authoritative source of information.
- Authority: This refers to the perceived credibility and trustworthiness of a website. A website seen as an authority on a particular subject is more likely to rank highly in search results.
- Trustworthiness refers to users' perceived level of trust in a website. A website perceived as trustworthy is more likely to be seen as an authoritative source of information and may rank higher in search results.

By demonstrating expertise, authority, and trustworthiness in their content and user interactions, websites can show Google that they provide value to searchers and something unique. It's important to note that Google's algorithms are constantly evolving, so staying up to date with the latest best practices and guidelines is essential to ensure that your website meets the E.A.T. principle.

Now that you know what SEO is, we will conduct keyword research in the next chapter to identify the best keywords to target for your website.

TWO
KEYWORD RESEARCH

This chapter will cover the importance of conducting keyword research and identifying the most relevant keywords for your website. And since the beginning of this year, there have been some incredible advances with some drawbacks. We'll look at it all.

WHY IS KEYWORD RESEARCH IMPORTANT?

Keyword research is essential in SEO because it helps you understand what terms and phrases people are searching for online and how competitive they are. By targeting the right keywords, you can increase the chances that the right audience will find your website.

HOW DO YOU CONDUCT KEYWORD RESEARCH

There are a few different ways to conduct keyword research, including:

1. Use a keyword research tool: Many tools can help you identify popular and relevant keywords for your

website. Some popular options include Google's Keyword Planner, SEMrush, and MOZ. In addition, there are also some recently developed AI options.

2. Look at your competitors: Analyzing the keywords your competitors are ranking for can give you ideas for terms to target on your website.

3. Consider your target audience: Think about the terms and phrases that your target audience might use to search for the types of books or topics you write about.

4. Use relevant long-tail keywords: Long-tail keywords are more specific and less competitive than shorter, more general terms. For example, "best-selling science fiction books" is a long-tail keyword more likely to be used by someone actively looking to purchase a science fiction book.

Before we go any further, we need to define some of these terms.

- Relevant Keywords: This should be an obvious answer, but these are keywords pertinent to the books that you write, and if you offer services to authors, the work that you do. We'll look at this even more in-depth in the companion course to this book.
- Volume: How many people are searching for this keyword every month? In other words, how many website visits does that mean, even if you are number one?
- Competitiveness, both organic and paid. How many people are trying to rank for this keyword, so how hard will it be for me to break in? How many people pay for ads for that keyword, and what does that cost?
- Long tail keywords: this is more like a sentence someone would type into a search bar, like the best sci-fi novel of 2023.

We'll discuss these keywords in more detail as we move through the topics in this book, but this is an excellent foundation to get you started.

SEARCHING MANUALLY FOR KEYWORDS

One of the cheapest and easiest ways to search for keywords is manually. How do you do that? The simplest way is to start typing things into Google or any other search engine.

We've all seen the auto-complete that comes up when you type something into a search engine. It's how we discovered that pdf is the most popular world religion.

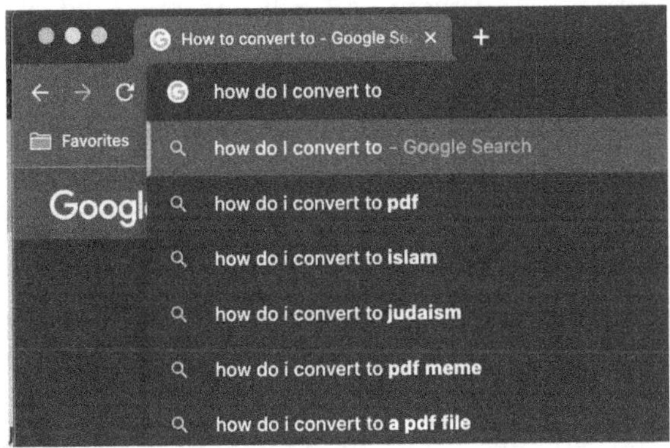

But seriously, this screenshot shows how popular this search is, which likely is good news for Adobe. Because this type of query shows us what people are searching for right now on Google or another search engine.

If we do the exact search with "romance novel" or romance authors, or any other genre, we will see what searchers are looking for. We're going to see patterns really quickly, patterns that can help us find keywords and long-tail phrases people are looking at.

Now, when we talk about search, we will talk mainly about Google, and if you are taking the SEO course that goes with this book, that is the example you will see most often. The reason is that for authors, at least at the moment, Google and Amazon are the two largest search engines we concern ourselves with.

CHANGES COMING IN SEARCH

"What about AI?" you ask legitimately. "How will that change search?" Well, the answer is actually more straightforward than you think. Search engines rely on ad revenue, and for those ads to show alongside organic results, there are only a few ways a search engine can change. Primarily, the results will still be keyword driven. And there will still be some kind of ranking algorithm.

Of course, as Google moves to more "conversational" answers, ranking might be more challenging. But the principles of SEO will stay the same unless there is a significant shift in how search engines make money.

STEPS TO DOING A MANUAL KEYWORD SEARCH

First, be sure you are in incognito mode or a private browsing window, one that is not influenced by your search history. This way, you see what an imaginary person with no search bias would see if they searched for the terms you are looking for.

This is the only way to see raw, organic results. But are they realistic? Well, only kind of. The reason is all of us have search history and biases, and the algorithm will take that into account automatically. However, if your audience is romance readers, that is a bias they will have if they search for books on Google (although they are more likely to do so on Amazon, but more on that later).

Second, start with a phrase related to your books and genre. We could start simply with "romance novels," for example. A list will come up:

- best romance novels for adults
- romance novels for teens
- romantic novels pdf
- best steamy romance novels
- contemporary romance
- romance novels
- best romance novels of all time
- historical romance novels
- best romance novels
- romance books for adults
- romance novels for women
- romance authors

This is quite simply a list of keywords. You can then take these keywords and start with the one closest to your book or insert other ideas to narrow them down. For example, if I do another search for "best historical steamy romance novels," I come up with another list:

- best historical steamy romance novels
- best steamy historical romance novels free online
- best steamy historical romance novels Kindle Unlimited
- best steamy historical romance authors
- best steamy historical Western romance novels
- best steamy historical romance books
- best steamy historical romance novels 2022
- best steamy historical romance novels Reddit
- best steamy historical romance novels 2021
- best steamy historical fiction

You can also look at the search results to see what is popular right now. Pride and Prejudice and The Notebook are always popular in the general romance category. But you will see things like Friends with Monsters and Dark Highlander topping the list in the steamy historical category.

Note also that when it comes to books, most of the results are organic, not paid. In other words, very few sponsored links are at the top of these searches. Because readers tend to search their favorite retailer for books, there is less competition in this space, at least for specific keywords, although we will examine that later, and you'll understand why.

Notice also that the retailers like Amazon and Barnes and Noble rank the highest in these categories, along with sites like Goodreads. After that, things that rank include lists of the "best of" categories you have searched, often followed by review sites.

Manual searches can be a time suck. You can keep refining and searching words until you have quite a list. This is where the keyword tools we will look at next come in. They automate that process and save you a lot of time. But even if you use those tools, even the best of them, it does not hurt to every now and then do a manual search, even if that is to develop a list you import into a tool that will broaden your search and help you refine your keyword list.

The principle is to determine what people are searching for and then use those keywords to get them to your website. For manual research, the final step is simply adding these keywords to a document or spreadsheet.

I almost always engage in manual keyword research like this before I turn to a tool. That way, I have a list to start with of what I know people are searching for right now. Try it yourself. It's excellent practice.

But once you have learned to do manual research, then it is time to turn to time-saving tools. We'll start by looking at AI.

USING AI FOR KEYWORD RESEARCH

As I wrote this book, something new came up: well, not new, but new to this space. Generative AI went from a tool available to only a few to one widely available and widely used. In fact, as of this writing, most marketers say they use AI daily or near daily to help them do their jobs.

But what does it mean for SEO, specifically keyword research? While we will touch on SEO for content generation, here we will talk about an area where it can be beneficial: keyword research.

But from the start, I will tell you that you need to use the other tools we talk about later in this course to verify the results you get. More on that in a moment. First, let's dive into AI for SEO Keyword Research.

WHAT IS GENERATIVE AI?

Let's debunk a myth right now. Generative AI, as we know it today, is not sentient. It does not have ideas or think for itself. Instead, it is a Large Language Model (LLM) that predicts an order of words or concepts based on the "training" it has received. This training often has come from several internet sources, documents, and other "training materials." For those who are complaining about "training A.I.," here is some news for you:

If you have written an email in Gmail, used Google Docs, filled out Google forms, used social media, published blogs online, owned a website, written other online content for clients, and a million more things, you have already worked to train A.I., including Google Bard, Open AI, and all of the other tools out there.

All content freely available on the web has been training these Large Language Models for years. And it is not going to stop anytime soon. If you are using A.I. in any capacity, you are helping train it.

But A.I. does not act with intent. The machine does not get up in the morning and decide to write a blog post or a novel, answer your questions, or even find your keywords. Also, because this is a predictive model and most A.I. training is only current until 2021-ish (with improvements coming all the time), the information it provides often needs to be updated, is factually wrong, or even made up.

This is why, as we will see, much of the generative written content is unusable without serious edits. At that point, you might as well write it yourself with a giant but.

The but is that generative A.I. can be good at creating outlines, but more importantly for this discussion, a list of keywords. How do you do that, though? There are many tools out there, and it can be confusing.

WHAT ABOUT ALL THOSE APPS AND EMERGING SOFTWARE?

Since Open AI essentially opened their API to developers, people are creating apps like crazy. Truth be told, it is relatively easy, but it can be expensive for users. More on that in a moment, but it is safe to say that any internet search right now will reveal dozens of tools, some worthwhile, some not, and many of which will not last.

But keep an eye on a website called AppSumo (see more details on the resources page on my website related to this book). They have all kinds of deals on emerging software, but it always is a gamble. If the software is successful and "makes it," you often get a lifetime license to something pretty cool. If it doesn't, you're out a few bucks.

Use caution with A.I. tools, however. Many are built on the Open AI platform, and it is expensive to use that platform, not because of the payouts to use the API but due to the computing power needed to power these LLMs. And with all the competition in emerging tools, some of those "lifetime deals" could be short-lived.

So, what do I recommend?

HOW DO I USE AI FOR KEYWORD RESEARCH?

Often the best way to get the most valuable information is to go to the source. My preference for developing keyword lists is to go right to Chat GPT (The OG Open AI software that took the world by storm), Google Bard, or Microsoft's Co0pilot (already active in some of their software).

Other programs we will review later in this section, related to keyword research also integrate AI features. Many of those tools will be improved by AI, but understand that it will come at a cost, so if you are using the "free" versions of them, you may not have all the functionality you need.

But that is true of Chat GPT and other LLMs as well. I used the paid version of Chap GPT, so I get access to the latest models and don't have limitations to how much data I can load or how many messages I can use in a day.

It's going to cost you something.

But the prompts are simple: here is one I used for the screenshot below. (More detail is shown in the SEO for authors online course):

"Show me a list of keywords for a mystery and thriller author website to improve search rankings and compete against similar websites."

Below are the results:

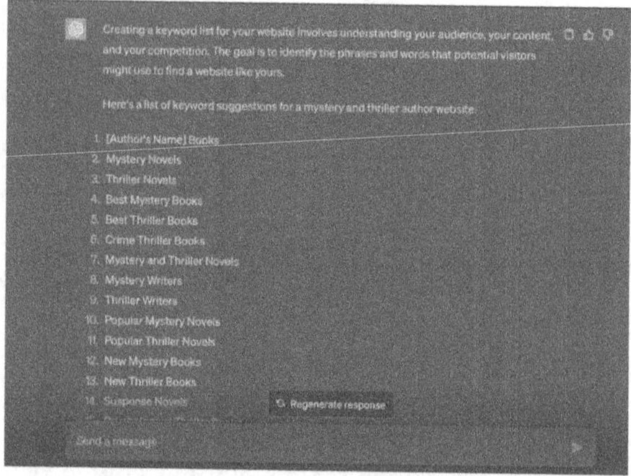

Overall, the response generated a list of 50 Keywords. Here they are:

Here's a list of keyword suggestions for a mystery and thriller author website:

1. [Author's Name] Books
2. Mystery Novels
3. Thriller Novels
4. Best Mystery Books
5. Best Thriller Books
6. Crime Thriller Books
7. Mystery and Thriller Novels
8. Mystery Writers
9. Thriller Writers
10. Popular Mystery Novels
11. Popular Thriller Novels

12. New Mystery Books
13. New Thriller Books
14. Suspense Novels
15. Psychological Thriller Books
16. Detective Novels
17. Best Crime Novels
18. Crime Fiction Authors
19. Mystery Series Books
20. Thriller Series Books
21. Mystery Book Recommendations
22. Thriller Book Recommendations
23. [Author's Name] Book Reviews
24. Upcoming Mystery Books
25. Upcoming Thriller Books
26. Award-Winning Mystery Novels
27. Award-Winning Thriller Novels
28. [Author's Name] Interviews
29. Murder Mystery Books
30. Spine-Chilling Thrillers
31. Books Like [Famous Author in the Same Genre]
32. Top Mystery Authors
33. Top Thriller Authors
34. Bestselling Mystery Novels
35. Bestselling Thriller Novels
36. Book Club Mystery Picks
37. Book Club Thriller Picks
38. Female Mystery Authors
39. Male Mystery Authors
40. Female Thriller Authors
41. Male Thriller Authors
42. Classic Mystery Novels
43. Classic Thriller Novels
44. Modern Mystery Novels
45. Modern Thriller Novels
46. [Author's Name] Book Signings

47. [Author's Name] New Releases

"Remember that while these are general suggestions, your best results will come from keywords that are most relevant to your website. Use tools like Google's Keyword Planner, SEMrush, or MOZ to identify high-volume, low-competition keywords. Also, incorporate local SEO strategies if the author frequently hosts events or signings in specific locations."

Some of these keywords do not work for me and my website, such as "female thriller authors" and others. And #31 would require some research and could develop into a whole host of keywords (how to rank for those will be revealed in coming chapters).

This list is just a start. Note the warning in quotes, put out there by Chat GPT: these are general suggestions, and it even offers a suite of tools you should use to vet these keywords. If you took this list, put it on your website, and just rolled with it, you would not get terrible results, but you would likely miss some opportunities.

What's next?

WHAT DO I DO WITH THE RESULTS?

This list, as stated above, is a good starting point. However, it is just that. Now I turn to the suite of tools we will discuss to ensure those keywords make sense for my website and my situation. You will have to do the same. We will outline logical steps that will lead you to a list that works for you.

Then we'll talk about why you might want to rank for more keywords than you think. But first, let's look at some other tools.

THREE
KEYWORD RESEARCH TOOLS

There are a ton of tools, both new and established, for doing keyword research. In this chapter, we will look at a few established and one new-ish software you can use for free.

All of them have paid versions, but the free versions are enough for most authors. However, as your career grows or you move to selling books and merchandise directly on your website, you may want to move to some more advanced tools and analytics.

In the meantime, here are some free tools to get you started.

GOOGLE KEYWORD PLANNER

Google's Keyword Planner is a free tool in the Google Ads platform. Here is the thing: Google wants your ads to succeed. If they are successful, you keep running them, and that is where Google and other search engines make the most of their money.

However, you don't have to run Google ads to use it, although your Google Ads account will have to be active. If you don't run ads for an extended period, Google will shut down your ads account for inactivity. Don't worry. You can reactivate it quickly enough, but if it has been a while, just be aware that you will need to do this.

There are a few different ways to use Google's Keyword Planner:

1. Identify popular and relevant keywords: The Keyword Planner allows you to enter a seed keyword or phrase like what I did with Chat GPT Above and see a list of related keywords, along with data on the search volume and competition level for each term. This is a part of vetting those keywords to ensure they work for your website and the books you write.

2. Research keyword trends: The Keyword Planner includes a feature that allows you to see how search volumes for specific keywords have changed over time. This can help you understand trends in keyword popularity and identify opportunities for targeting new or emerging keywords. It can also help you with seasonal keywords: if you have a Christmas romance, you can see when the best times of year to market might be. (Hint, take a look at July romance authors)

3. Find new keyword ideas: The seed keywords you entered, whether you got them from Chat GPT or your manual research, can give you new ideas from the list the Google keyword planner creates. You can then take that list and use items on it as seed keywords of their own. This allows you to make more lists, companion lists if you will, and can literally give you hundreds of potential keywords to target.

4. Create several keyword lists: You can import keywords from a spreadsheet or elsewhere and build extended lists, have Google Keywords create and store those lists, and more. Remember that if your account is deactivated

for inactivity, you might want to keep those lists elsewhere.

In fact, I recommend that you download and store any keyword lists somewhere other than the tool you are using. Although keywords can change over time, for most authors, that is rare. Once you have a good list, it will be time to go to work ranking for those and other terms.

Pros: A FREE Tool. Google Keyword Planner will not cost you anything, and Google is always actively adding AI and other features. You do have to keep your ads account active to continue using it, but that isn't a problem for most people.

Cons: There is a steep learning curve, which can be time-consuming. The dashboard and tools for Google Keyword Planner are not 100% intuitive, and it takes some time to master and understand. While this book will give you a good foundation for understanding terms, you'll still have some work to do.

Fortunately, Google Keyword Planner is not the only tool out there, and many have free options for you to explore.

UBERSUGGEST

Ubersuggest is a tool created by Neil Patel, a well-known SEO guru who runs an agency and has been in the game for a long time. He created this tool as an alternative to the others available. And one of his focuses is on content. The tool has all kinds of uses, but one of my favorites is the content ideas it spells out for you.

As you will see, other tools can also give you content ideas, but if you are going to pay for a tool, Ubersuggest is one of the more affordable options. It can still:

The parts include:

- A keyword overview, like that of Google Keyword Planner, and some other tools we will look at, you enter a seed or starter keyword and get a list of related keywords.
- Keyword ideas, or a keyword discovery tool, helps you find related keywords you might have yet to consider.
- Keywords by traffic: How much traffic do these keywords get?
- Similar websites: how does your website compare to others who are ranking for similar keywords?
- Content ideas: Ideas for content you could create that will help your site rank for your chosen keywords.

The best way to use Ubersuggest is to enter your website and the keywords you want to rank for and then monitor how you are doing in those areas. To really benefit from this, of course, you will need the paid version of the tool.

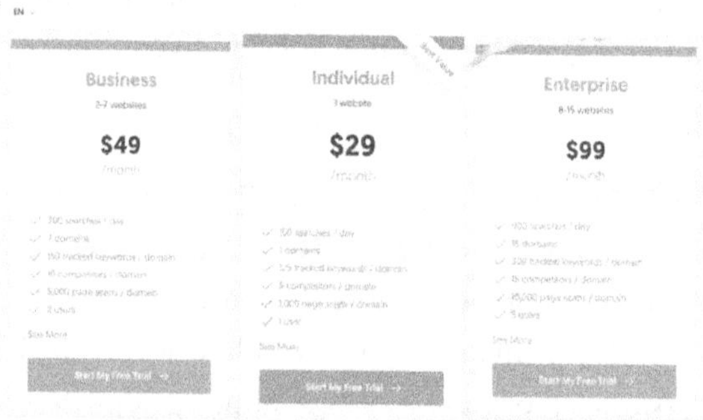

As of this writing, this is the pricing structure. The good news is that as an author, you can probably subscribe for a few months, get a baseline of keywords and how your efforts are working, and then cancel your subscription. This is not a tool you are likely to need all the time.

The SEO for Authors course has an even more in-depth dive into each tool, including this one.

SEMRUSH

SEMrush is a popular all-in-one marketing tool that provides a range of features for keyword research, including:

1. Keyword overview: like other keyword research tools, the SEMrush Keyword Overview tool allows you to enter a seed keyword or phrase and see a list of related keywords, along with data on the search volume and competition level for each.
2. Keyword Magic tool: The Keyword Magic tool can help you discover new keywords you may not have thought of, similar to the keyword idea tool in Ubersuggest.
3. Keyword difficulty tool: The Keyword Difficulty tool allows you to see the estimated difficulty level of ranking for a specific keyword based on factors such as the number and quality of links pointing to the pages that currently rank for that keyword. This can help you understand the level of competition for a particular keyword and determine whether it is a feasible target for your website.
4. Keyword gap tool: The Keyword Gap tool allows you to compare the keywords for which two or more websites are ranking. This can help you identify opportunities to target new keywords and gain a competitive advantage in the search results.

This tool has free options that are enough for authors to get started, and like Ubersuggest, it has some inexpensive plans that you can easily afford for a few months to get your SEO plan started. You can also monitor your site and how you are doing with this tool, including the free version, but there are other tools you can use for that purpose, as you will discover later in the book.

Another note: all these tools will reveal different things and give you different keyword results. That does not mean one is wrong and another is right: instead, it means there are a variety of approaches to keyword research, and using a variety of them will give you the best results.

Pros: A free and relatively cheap tier for authors.

Cons: It can be a rabbit hole and a time suck (data is fascinating). Also, if you are not careful, this can lead you down the wrong keyword path, away from your area of expertise related to your books, and find you ranking for things irrelevant to your subject matter.

As with any tool, try this out, and see if it resonates with you.

USING MOZ FOR KEYWORD RESEARCH

Moz is another powerful tool for keyword research that provides a range of features, some similar to the tools we have looked at already and some that are different. Moz offers a full suite of SEO tools for free, and we will look at those throughout the book. But for the moment, we will focus on the Keyword Explorer. It gives you some great information, including:

- Volume and difficulty: How many people are searching for this keyword, and how hard is it to rank for?
- Organic CTR Rate: this tells you the percentage of people clicking on ads vs. those choosing to click on organic traffic. This is a helpful metric whether you run ads or not and can help you decide if you should.
- Keyword suggestions: among the free tools, this gives you more recommendations than any of them, even if

there is not much detail about each. This is a great list to take to other tools or to explore further on Moz.

- SERP Results: this shows you who is ranking for what keyword. It can give you an idea of what the competition is like out there and how you can improve your chance of ranking, if at all.

This is one of my favorite tools, but it has pros and cons.

Pros: A free and relatively cheap tier for authors. There are many tools you can access for free.

Cons: There are limits on the free tool, and if you are not careful, you can run out of searches quickly, leaving you in a lurch if you are trying to do some intense research. This can be overcome by combining Moz with other tools.

That's all the specific tools we're going to explore. There are a lot of others out there, but these are the leading players, at least at the moment. They'll get you the keywords you need to get started on your website.

Because that is where we are headed, in the next lesson, we will discuss optimizing your website's SEO content by incorporating these keywords into your website's title tags, meta descriptions, and body content.

In other words, where do all these keywords go so that Google (and your web visitors) see them?

FOUR
ON-PAGE OPTIMIZATION

What is on-page optimization? On-page optimization refers to the process of optimizing individual web pages in order to rank higher and earn more relevant traffic in search engine results pages (SERPs). This includes optimizing the content and HTML source code of each page on your website, including everything from the home pages and the calendar to blog posts.

What is a SERP?

We defined this before, but it bears repeating: a search engine results page (SERP) is a page displayed by a search engine in response to a query. It includes a list of results that the search engine considers relevant, along with sponsored ads and other features such as maps and images. If you want only images, you can search for just visual results; the same is true of videos, news, books, and more.

The results on a SERP are usually ranked in order of relevance, with the most relevant results appearing at the top of the page. The ranking of results on a SERP is determined by the search engine's algorithms, which consider factors such as the relevance and quality of the content, the number and quality of links pointing to the page, and the presence of structured data.

SERPs can vary depending on the search engine and the query type. For example, a SERP for a local search query may include a map with local businesses, while a SERP for an image search query may include a grid of images.

HOW TO OPTIMIZE YOUR WEBSITE'S CONTENT FOR SEO

Here are a few tips for optimizing your website's content for SEO:

1. Use your keyword research to identify the most relevant keywords for each website page.
2. Incorporate these keywords into the title tag and meta description for each page. The title tag is the text that appears in the search results, and the meta description is a summary of the page's content that also appears in the search results.
3. Use header tags (H1, H2, etc.) to structure the content of your page and make it easier for search engines to understand the main topics and subtopics on the page.
4. Use internal and external links to enhance the user experience and provide additional information for readers. This can also help improve the authority of your website.
5. Use alt text to describe images on your website. This helps search engines understand the content of the images and can also improve accessibility for visually impaired users.
6. Make sure your website is mobile-friendly and loads quickly. With the increasing use of mobile devices to

access the internet, it's crucial to ensure your website is easily accessible and user-friendly on various devices.

Of course, in this general advice section, we skipped over a lot of detail related to each type and placement of keywords, so let's look at each in depth.

TITLE TAGS AND META-DESCRIPTIONS

The title tag and meta description are essential elements of on-page SEO, as they help search engines understand the content and context of your website pages. Here's how you can set the title tags and meta descriptions for your website pages:

1. Identify the target keyword or phrase: Determine the primary keyword or phrase you want to target for each page. This should be a relevant, high-quality keyword that accurately describes the content of that page related to the audience you want to reach. It should also be associated with the overall keywords you want your website to rank for.
2. Write a compelling title tag: The title tag is the text that appears in your page's search results and browser tab. It should be concise and descriptive and include the target keyword. This title tag should be at most 60 characters long, as longer titles may be truncated in the search results. In other words, keep it brief but long enough to have meaning.
3. Write a clear and concise meta description: The meta description is a short summary of the page's content that appears in the search results below the title tag. It should be accurate, informative, and include the target keyword. It should be at most 160 characters long but a manageable length, too. Be sure there is enough

information for the searcher to determine if the result is relevant to what they searched for.

By setting clear and concise title tags and meta descriptions, you can help search engines understand the content and context of your website pages and how they relate to and support the overall message of your website.

The most important thing to do when creating content is to keep your target audience in mind. What matters to them, and what are they searching for? Can you offer them information that other websites do not, or can you provide better information or something more entertaining?

We'll talk more about writing content in a bit, but for now, we want to focus on where and how to create good title tags and meta descriptions.

YOUR FOCUS KEYWORD(S)

This is Just a note to say that setting your focus keywords is the best way to ensure your title and metadata fit your overall strategy. Remember above that we mentioned the main keyword related to the post or page you are working on, which should be relevant to the post and your overall site. This keyword goes in the "focus keyword" area of the tools we will look at.

This helps you determine if your title and metadata align with your topic. Remember, you are writing these two things with a dual purpose. One is to tell Google what your site is about, and the second is to show the person searching Google, your reader, what your site is about.

The ideal title and meta description will appeal to both.

Example: Setting the Title Tags and Meta Description in WordPress Using Yoast SEO

In WordPress, you can set your website pages' title tags and meta descriptions using the Yoast SEO plugin. There are both free and pro versions, and it is one of the most common plugins writers use on their websites to check how they are doing with SEO. As we will see, it is not the only plugin to do that, but it is good.

Here are the steps to get it active on your WordPress site. If you are taking the SEO for Authors course, there is a detailed walkthrough on this and other SEO tools inside. Yoast makes it pretty easy, though: the interface is a simple one, and so is the installation. We'll talk about this in the context of WordPress first and then add some details on other platforms after.

Installation:

1. Install and activate the Yoast SEO plugin: Go to your WordPress dashboard's "Plugins" section and click "Add New." Search for "Yoast SEO" and install and activate the plugin.
2. If you want the features of Yoast SEO Pro, set up your account and payment method. However, many writers do well with the free version.

Once you are in the plugin, add a post or a new page to your website. You will see various options for adding title tags and metadata at the bottom of that interface and the editor you are using.

But this is an important point: you must have your content created first, at least in most cases. You don't want to write your content in WordPress but in another editor or software (I use Word, but Google Docs and others also work.

1. Set the title of your post and add the text or any other images to the page or post on your website. Be sure you are still in the "Edit Post" area.

2. Set the title tag and meta description: Scroll down to the "Yoast SEO" box and enter your title tag and meta description in the designated fields.

3. When your title or meta description fits the required parameters, the line they are on will turn green. That is your indication that you have done things correctly.

4. If the description is too short, the line will be yellow. It will be red if it is too long, indicating that the title or description will be "truncated" or cut off by search engines. You can see this in the next step.

5. Preview the title tag and meta description: The Yoast SEO plugin includes a "Snippet Preview" feature that lets you see how your title tag and meta description will appear in the search results. This can show you what your information will look like, so you can modify it for both appearance and accuracy.

We will talk about the overall SEO score and recommendations from Yoast as we move through this part of the book, but for now, that is how you set the title tag and meta description using this plugin.

USING SMARTSEO TO SET TITLE AND META DESCRIPTION DATA

Another option for a plugin is SmartSEO. It is part of a suite of plugins called WPMU Dev. But it is a handy tool, just as powerful as Yoast, and with some exciting features.

But it works almost the same way, at least for this part of our discussion. You will see a box at the bottom of your editor with SEO Analysis as the title. Underneath that, you will see a button that says, "Edit Meta." This is where you will set your title tag and meta description.

The interface is like Yoast in that colors will indicate if you are "good to go" for the title and meta description length. There is also an overall SEO score we will talk about as we move forward.

WIX, SHOPIFY, SQUARE, AND OTHER WEBSITE BUILDERS

I'll only touch on these briefly for two reasons: the first is that they are not the usual choices for authors for several reasons, and second, they all have similar SEO tools or plugins, and they work about the same way.

"Free" site builders like Wix tend to be less powerful, or you end up paying for plugins that you can get for free on a WordPress platform (and there are many more of them). As of this writing, just over 80% of websites are built on some WordPress base. You can put many builders on top of those, as you will learn later in this book.

However, without going down too deep of a rabbit hole, I'll say that if you use a different builder, you will still have similar SEO options, and while they may look a little different, the intent is the same. Even the free versions will have some technique to set your SEO data.

You may have to explore those on your own.

If you are a designer and coding your website using HTML, CSS, or some combination of those, there are other ways to set this information as well. The point is that no matter the method, you need a focus keyword, a title tag, and a meta description that tells search engines what your page or post is about.

WHAT IF I DON'T SET TITLE TAGS AND META DESCRIPTIONS?

If you do not set title tags and meta descriptions, search engines will create them for you. The title tag will be the title of your page: this can be okay, but there are other times when it does not work.

The meta description will just be the first 160 characters of your page or post. That can be bad, and most of the time it is. While you start with a clear introduction, that is probably not optimized for SEO.

You can and should control this for the best SEO results. Remember, your goal is to get more web visitors interested in joining your email list, consuming your content, and hopefully eventually buying your books.

The other thing you can control on your website? The content on your page. For the purposes of this book, we will start with header tags.

USING HEADER TAGS (H1, H2, ETC.)

Header tags, also known as HTML headings, are used to organize and structure the content of a webpage. There are six levels of header tags, ranging from H1 (the most important) to H6 (the least important). Here are a few ways to use header tags for on-page SEO optimization:

1. By using header tags to divide your content into sections and sub-sections, you can make it easier for users to read and understand the content of your page. This can improve the user experience and increase the likelihood that users will stay on your page longer.

2. Include your target keywords in header tags: This signals search engines and reveals your page's main topics and themes to them. This can help improve the relevance and ranking of your page for keywords related to the post and the overall theme of your site.

3. It's essential to use header tags hierarchically, with H1 tags used for the main heading and H2 tags used for subheadings, etc. This helps search engines understand the structure and hierarchy of the content on your page. Most of the time, you will only go down to H3 tags unless you write a long-form article over 1500 words or so.

4. It's also important to avoid using header tags to stuff keywords into your content. Search engines see this as spammy and can actually harm your ranking. Instead, use header tags to naturally and effectively organize and structure your content. Your headings do not need to look natural; they must be natural. If they feel "wrong" to your readers, they will leave your site and possibly never return.

Think of your header tags as the outline of your pages or blog posts. Your content is the meat of the article and what really matters. It keeps you and the readers of your website on track. The more specific each page and post, the better.

Readers tend to have short attention spans, although there are different types of web visitors you can direct your content to. We will talk about that more shortly. For now, let's turn to another part of your content: internal and external links.

INTERNAL AND EXTERNAL LINKS

Internal and external links are an essential part of on-page SEO, as they help search engines understand the content and context of your website and can improve the visibility and ranking of your pages in the search results.

Internal links create what we call a content island. The more content you have related to other content on your site, the more important search engines think your site is and the more authority you have on the topic. It also gives your readers a place to go on your website when they want more information. This keeps them on your site longer and makes it likely they will buy.

External links provide what we call a good "link neighborhood." This is defined by the authority of the sites you link to. So instead of linking to Wikipedia or similar sites, link to legitimate news sites, education institutions, scientific articles, and sources considered reliable.

Often, that will result in high-authority sites linking to yours, which builds your site authority. More on link building in another chapter, but for now, the principle is this: the better sites you link to, the easier it will be to get good sites to link to yours.

Use descriptive anchor text. Anchor text is the visible text of a link that users click on to access the linked page. It's important to use text that accurately reflects the content of the linked page, as this can help search engines understand the context and relevance of the link. It can also help the site you are linking to, as your site can help build its authority. It's kind of a win-win.

However, do the same for your internal links. Those keywords can tell search engines how your content is related and why linking to it (and ranking it well) is important.

Use a mix of internal and external links. Links are like salt: too many, and you'll spoil your content. Too little, and it won't resonate with your readers or search engines.

Before we leave the idea of links, let's address anchor text a little more in-depth.

ANCHOR TEXT AND WHY IT MATTERS

Anchor text is the visible text of a link that users click on to access the linked page. In the context of on-page SEO, anchor text is essential because it helps search engines understand what the link is about. Ideally, anchor text can and should include your focus keywords.

However, the anchor text must accurately reflect the linked page's content. Don't force your keywords in here. Use natural anchor text above all. If you use anchor text that is unrelated or spammy, it can actually harm your rankings if it is at all suspect or even deliberately wrong.

Anchor text plays a significant role in on-page SEO. But as we said above, it must be natural.

Before we move to off-page optimization, we will take a moment to talk about content.

FIVE

CONTENT AND TYPES OF WEB VISITORS

For a moment, we need to examine how to create content for your pages and posts, essentially the words, images, and videos on your website. This is what the searcher comes for and what keeps them coming back.

Remember that while we create content for Google and other search engines, the real reason we create it is for users who visit our website and eventually purchase our books. That is the audience and the goal we need to keep in mind.

THE TYPES OF WEB VISITORS

First and most important is understanding the types of web visitors. There are three distinct groups you will want to create content for and another that, while you may not create content directly for, you should be aware of as you create blog posts.

They are defined as streakers, strollers, and studiers. The fourth group is researchers, but they are by far the smallest group on the web, and while it can help to have some content that appeals to them, most of the time, content created for studiers is deep enough for most authors. Most of the time, you are creating content for streakers and strollers, by far the most significant web audiences.

STREAKERS

Streakers are those internet browsers who land on a page, look for whatever they came for, and then move on to something else. They probably read the headers of your article, and if you can interest them with those, they may read more (turning them into a stroller, as we will see in a moment).

The idea of streakers is to create content with strong headers and clear calls to action so that the web visitor sees what they want, is engaged by it, and takes the action you want them to. We'll talk more about a call to action next and how that plays a role in SEO, but for now, understand that streakers want to find the information they are looking for fast.

They are the headline and heading readers. They make decisions quickly and generally based on instinct rather than a lot of information. You usually have one shot at a streaker – they don't shop around and return to buy something later. The first few sentences or words of your book blurb, blog post, or sales pitch must grab them. Otherwise, they are often gone forever.

Short-form blog content, video, and captivating images all contribute to getting and keeping their attention and getting them to take the next step.

You can turn a streaker into a stroller if your headlines, headers, or calls to action are strong enough. But it can be done if you can both grab and keep their attention.

STROLLERS

Instead of racing through the internet like their streaker brethren, strollers are strolling through, doing a bit of browsing and window shopping. They may even be looking to make a purchase, although they generally have yet to learn what they want to buy. They are looking for options.

In the case of books, they are looking for entertainment that will satisfy their tastes and even their mood. They need more information than you can include in a headline or header so that they will read the entire article. They may skim parts that could be more interesting to them, but they are looking for bullet points that include information like benefits, pros, cons, etc. We will talk in the next section (briefly) about how a "problem-solving" approach to selling your work can produce a lot of incentive to buy.

This is not to say that your website or blog is all about selling. Not at all. You are looking to build relationships with your readers, and to do that, you need to connect with them. Sometimes a page or blog post is just designed to keep them coming back and reading more. That's the only call to action you need.

But the better your relationship, especially with strollers, the more likely they are to become true fans and consume not only what you offer for free on your website but your books as well. These fans will pay full price for your work, purchase it directly from you, and support you in other ways.

For a stroller, keywords and engaging content between the headers are important. The first sentence of each paragraph should make them want to stay and read the rest. Hooks, just like you use in fiction, should keep them reading from sentence to sentence, section to section.

Short to medium-form content works well for this group, and video and images are a definite plus.

The idea is to turn your casual stroller into a studier.

STUDIERS

Is studier a word? It is now. A studier doesn't just want to know the surface but wants to go deeper and truly understand what you are writing about, who you are, your work, and even the research behind it.

They want to dive deep, but not too deep. They may follow links in your blog posts to discover what you referenced and why. They may ask questions in the comments or even email you. They leave detailed reviews and enjoy the cerebral side of reading.

The studier is your ultimate fan, and they often make good "beta readers." Even if they don't want to go to that level, they will offer you feedback and voraciously consume what you create.

Your content still must be well written, but the "punchier" aspect can be toned down a bit, and they are here for longer form content.

RESEARCHERS

The final type of internet searcher is a researcher. The researcher wants to go even deeper than the studier. In the case of authors, these are often other authors or aspiring writers. They want to know and understand your process and see "under the hood." How did you do this thing or that one? Can they do the same thing or something similar?

If you write non-fiction, this can also be an actual academic researcher. They want to see your sources, research, and verify your outcomes and opinions. They are deep divers. This is the smallest group of internet searchers, and sadly may not even be interested in your fiction work. Targeting this group works best for non-fiction authors who are a part of academia or writing on high-level topics.

A call to action may not be valuable for these readers. They will either buy or not based on their research, which could include visiting several websites and looking at the work of various authors.

For the purposes of SEO, remember that three primary types of searchers will visit your blog or website and that the two most common are streakers and strollers. Your titles, headings, and content will speak to them differently, as will your calls to action.

This means that although it is essential for your content to include keywords, it must also include engaging hooks and have a style that appeals to searchers and search engines.

In general, clear, concise, and focused writing that stays on track with keywords and subject matter will work better with both search engines and people.

This brings us to calls to action and how they impact SEO.

SIX

CALLS TO ACTION

As we talk about types of visitors, it is crucial that we still keep keywords in mind, but not just related to content. Those keywords are essential, but are they relevant to your call to action? That depends on what you want your web visitor to do.

And that depends on the type of content you are creating and its purpose.

There are three purposes for your website:

- To engage with readers, both ongoing readers and new to you readers
- To get readers and preferably book buyers to sign up for your newsletter.
- To get readers to purchase your books or other merchandise from your site.

Most of your content will fall into one of these categories. They include:

- Landing pages are designed for a single purpose or call to action. This is usually to subscribe to your newsletter (and get your reader magnet or another freebie) or to make a purchase.
- Regular pages can have a variety of purposes but usually include either signing up for your newsletter or making a purchase. The difference is that these pages often contain multiple calls to action, enabling users to navigate and discover the rest of your website.
- Blog posts are usually designed to engage with readers, get them to pay attention to your content, and keep coming back for more. It allows them to interact with you between purchases and book releases.

Let's look at each of these in detail.

LANDING PAGES

Landing pages are designed for one purpose and often do not contain your website's navigation menu. They direct the user to do one thing: sign up for your newsletter or make a purchase, but usually not both. Both the keywords and call to action are narrowly focused. Really, the user is faced with two choices: take the action you want them to or close the page and navigate away.

This is powerful because they must choose to say "no" and navigate away or say yes. There is no option to say maybe. You see these pages often when you click on a paid ad. Usually, you target a single keyword or phrase, reflected in your page title, headings, and call-to-action buttons.

Search engines and your users will clearly know what this page is for. Sometimes your email management or customer management software will even allow you to create landing pages on their platform.

This can be both a good idea (it is easy) or not so good because you have less access to analytics that tell you where the web traffic came from, click-through and conversion rates, and more. We'll address that in the analytics lesson later, but it's not a bad idea to start thinking about this now.

REGULAR WEB PAGES

These are pages like your home page, a series page, or something similar. They are not landing pages, as the user has the option to look at your navigation menu and move around your website, but pages other than your home page are usually focused as well.

For example, your home page is the gateway to your website. There are usually links to all kinds of things, including various pages, newsletter signups, and more. If you are a new author, your home page may not have a lot of options, but if you are a seasoned writer with multiple books or even series and various formats like audio and special editions or even merchandise, your home page will offer more options.

But a regular webpage might also be a series page. It would offer navigation to the books in that series, including descriptions, reviews, where to purchase them, and more. While a reader could navigate to another series, that would involve them returning to your menu and making that choice.

This is an excellent place to offer your reader magnet for that series in exchange for a newsletter signup or a bundle deal on print books if they purchase from your website.

The point is that while there is a focus, rather than the single purpose a landing page has, there may be a few purposes to your regular web pages.

BLOG POSTS

Blog posts are even more specific. They also have a purpose: to inform the reader, entertain them, and entice them to engage with your content. This can be a good place for a call to action to a book or series related to the post or an invitation to join your email list for more related content.

But the purpose of a blog post is generally not a call to action. Instead, it is an engagement tool. This should be the least sales-focused of your pages. Your reader should come away feeling satisfied just to have consumed the content, and most often, should feel inspired to read more of the content on your blog as a result.

This does not mean you can't have a call to action, but it should be "soft" rather than a "hard" call to action on your landing page.

Blogs can be short, medium, or long, either high level (for streakers and some strollers), a little more in-depth for strollers and some studiers, or long-form and deep, designed for studiers and researchers. Remember that your primary goal is a mix of content with some appeal for each but an emphasis on streakers and strollers.

A call to action is great, but remember your keywords and what action you want the web visitor to take.

Now that we understand a call to action and what it is for, let's look at other ways you structure your content.

SEVEN

CREATING AND STRUCTURING CONTENT

Of course, you can't have a call to action without content to insert it into, and there are three common types of web content and a few less common types.

- Written content like web pages and blog posts we talked about in the last section.
- Photos to break up and enhance the written content
- Video content that goes with written content or stands alone

Audio content is a less common type of content, except on podcast websites. However, most podcast consumers listen to podcasts on another platform like Apple, Spotify, or another app. These pages usually direct readers to those platforms with written content while also providing the ability for web visitors to listen on the site as well.

But one of the most common questions I get from authors is, "What do I write about?" Here are some answers.

WHAT SHOULD I WRITE ABOUT?

Remember our ongoing example of the attorney/BBQ Chef? That is an example of what not to do, but what do you do? What topics are appropriate?

First, look at your keywords. What are you trying to rank for? If that is romance related, then your content should be, too. You can write about how romance novels can improve your love life, how fictional romance relates to real-life dating and more.

But you can go beyond that. You can do romance novel reviews, movie reviews, list top romantic date night locations in various cities, romantic travel, date ideas (inspired by your series, maybe?), or something about the culture depicted in your romance novels.

For example, if you are writing hockey romance, you can talk about hockey, romance, and what romance actually looks like for a hockey player. You can interview them, their girlfriends, or their spouses and talk about romance and athletes in general. What do relationships look like for real?

This is, of course, just one example. You can add all kinds of related things to your website, including:

- Character profiles: include profiles or side stories for your characters, especially minor ones readers may want to know more about.
- Setting deep dives: tell us something about each setting where your books take place. This can also include the time period if you are writing historical fiction.
- Profession deep dives: what does your character do for a living? Tell the readers more about it. Interview someone who does that job, or you can interview your character and let them answer. It can be fun and informative for both you and your readers.

You can write about your writing process, but a brief warning here: that is more interesting to other writers than to your readers, especially if you go deep into the workings of a writer. Also, avoid:

- Political topics, unless they relate to your work
- The same for religion, unless you are writing religious fiction or the topic relates more broadly to your stories
- Topics that are too personal. It is excellent that your readers want to get to know you but don't give them tools to stalk you online or even in real life. Keep a public persona, but unless the topics also relate directly to your fiction, avoid revealing too much

There are exceptions to these rules, especially regarding non-fiction, but be careful either way. You can quickly alienate a large part of your audience by delving into these topics.

This also does not mean that authors should not stand for causes: we should all be against the banning of books (even if we disagree with the topics of those books), should be in favor of authors being treated well and paid fairly for their work, and should have an interest in the equal treatment of writers and their stories regardless of race, gender, sexual orientation, religious preference, and more.

But some polarizing topics in both politics and religion should be "off limits" if you are going to be a public personality, and caution is always crucial. Ask several people if they find something offensive. If they do find something offensive, try to discover why. It could be a personal preference you could ignore or something you want to change in your writing.

Either way, choose your topics carefully to fit not only your keywords but the message and tone you want your books to convey.

HOW DO I STRUCTURE MY CONTENT?

Your content should be structured just like you see this book and various blogs structured. You should:

- Have titles that are eye-catching but accurately reflect what your content is about.
- Have headings that are engaging and tell the reader what is next.
- Use headings in a hierarchy so the reader and search engines know what is important in your content.
- Use short paragraphs to keep readers engaged and avoid the "wall of text" website look.
- Use bullet points and numbered lists to break up your text as well.
- Use photos and videos as needed (see sections below in a moment)
- Spread keywords evenly and naturally throughout your headings and content.

Like your content itself, the structure serves two purposes: it tells search engines what keywords to pay attention to and the topic or topics they are related to. The structure does the same for readers but also keeps them reading and engaged by mixing up the appearance of the content and showing them the most relevant information in an engaging way.

Study blogs and articles you like. Try to determine why you like them and why they work for you. Then imitate that with your own content.

Even though we've kind of already covered this, let's revisit where to put keywords.

WHERE DO I PUT KEYWORDS?

Keywords go everywhere: your title, headings, and content. However, the key is to avoid keyword stuffing. What does that mean?

In 2017 a guy created a post that essentially consisted of a bunch of filler words surrounded by the words "Super Bowl" repeated over and over again. For a few brief minutes (about 40), he outranked the actual Super Bowl website on search engines. This was due to an old practice called keyword stuffing, and it was just that: you put the keyword you want to rank for everywhere in your post, and with the most mentions of that keyword, your site will rank pretty high in search.

Except that does not work anymore, and that guy? When Google discovered his prank, he got his site delisted from Google. Forever. Now, the likelihood is, his goal was to outrank everything for a few moments for fame or whatever. The website he used probably didn't matter to him the way yours does to you.

Your keywords should occur naturally in sentences, headings, and throughout your pages or blog posts. Don't force them in but do use them as you are able. Because it works. Remember earlier in the book when I told you that even a lower-domain website can rank for a keyword over a higher-ranking one? I know because I did it.

When the Kingsman: The Golden Circle movie was in development, Old Forrester created a whiskey called "The Statesman" that would be featured in the movie. I learned about it and was able to publish an article a few hours before Forbes broke the same story. So for those few hours, one of my websites ranked above Forbes for this little article: https:// unboundnorthwest.com/kingsman-golden-circle-statesman-whisky-will-reality/

Included in the short-form piece was a video (the trailer for the movie), images (also from the movie), and some very strategic keywords.

When Forbes released their article on the same topic, it took them a couple of hours to outrank my little website because I was the first. It was a small victory, and that post got traffic for quite a while simply because of the topic and keywords.

That aside, go to your favorite author's website. Look at their blog. When you read an article, ask yourself what they are trying to rank for, and look to see if it fits their brand. Look at their regular pages and ask yourself the same thing.

Then use that to inform your own SEO and content strategy.

PHOTOS AND ALT TEXT

As promised earlier, here is a note on photos and alt text. Alt text is an accessibility trait of images that tells a reader who cannot see the photo on your website what that photo is about. But it also tells search engines what it is about. Although search engines now can "see" photos when they crawl your website, that was not always the case. This is why it is important to include alt text: not only for those who are visually impaired but for the "spiders" who crawl your website.

The alt text should accurately describe the photo but, if possible, should also include the keywords you are trying to rank for. This means the image should be relevant to the page or post it is attached to, or at least that section of the page.

However, even if for some reason it is not directly related, always add alt text to your images, as this makes your website ADA-compliant, another essential element in creating content.

VIDEO CONTENT: ANALYTICS AND EASE OF VIEWING

Finally, in some cases, you may create video content related to your pages or blog posts, whether these are book trailers, explainer videos, or other content. Either way, keywords are important. Make sure the video is related.

But where should you host those videos? You can put them on YouTube, Vimeo, or a similar platform and then embed them on your website. You may have access to some analytics as a result, but you can get more information if you self-host your videos either on your site or your own hosting platform.

We'll talk about that more in the analytics section, but to put it simply, the more control you have over where and how the content is hosted and shared, the better you will be able to see the value of creating it and how the SEO and metadata behind it are impacting both your website and your bottom line.

Okay. We have covered content creation rather thoroughly now, and we're ready to move on, this time to Off-Page Optimization. Let's dive right in.

EIGHT

OFF-PAGE SEO OPTIMIZATION

What is off-page optimization? Off-page optimization refers to the process of improving the visibility and authority of a website through activities that take place outside of the website itself. This can include building links from other websites, generating social media shares, and earning positive reviews and mentions.

BUILDING LINKS

One of the most effective off-page optimization techniques is building links from other websites to your own. When a website links to your site, it signals to search engines that your website is a credible and trustworthy source of information. This can help improve your website's ranking and visibility in search results.

To build links, you can either reach out to other websites and ask them to link to your site or work to earn those links naturally. It's important to focus on receiving or earning high-quality, relevant links from reputable websites rather than trying to acquire a large quantity of low-quality links.

The process of building links is referred to in SEO as Link Building.

COMMON LINK-BUILDING TECHNIQUES

The key to link building is keywords and ensuring that the links that point to your site have a relevant context or something that is at least tangentially related. Early in my freelance career, I got a lot of backlinks by having a link in my bio to my website. This was often a "naked link," where the anchor text was my website URL. I had a lot of "my website" anchor text, but then I started to do some new things.

If I were writing on a topic related to a particular site, I would create a blog post on my site related to that same topic and link that way. This is one of the most common methods of link building, but it is by far not the only one.

Below is a list of a few of them, and we will take a deeper look at each and how they work for authors.

1. Content marketing: As stated above, one of the most common ways to build links is to create high-quality, relevant, and engaging content that other websites want to link to. By creating valuable content that addresses the needs and interests of your target audience (a.k.a. your readers), you can attract natural links from other websites that find your content valuable and want to share it with their own audiences. You can either earn these links or even ask websites to link to yours.

2. Guest blogging: Guest blogging is an effective way to ask for links to your site. You give the site owner an article (or even sometimes get paid for it) on a website in your industry or niche. By doing this, you also establish yourself as an authority in your field.

3. Broken link building: This method involves identifying broken links on other websites and offering to replace them with a link to a page or blog post on your website. This is not common for writers: you have to use special tools to check for broken links on other sites, find the contact information for the site owner, and email them with an opportunity to use your link instead. More on this below.

4. Resource page link building: This method involves identifying resource pages on other websites relevant to what you write and offering to include a link to your website on those pages. If you write books for authors, this can consist of links placed on other writing sites. If you are an authority on the topic (fiction or non-fiction) you write about, you can also use this same strategy, linking to resources you have created on your site.

Remember, the quality and relevance of your links are more important than the quantity. The more authoritative site you can get to link to your website and content, the better. However, quantity matters as well. Don't turn down a link to your site from another one that is "good" but not great. A lot of links make a difference as well.

A note here: some sites exist just for people to put links on and sometimes link to their own group of sites. This is not always a good practice, but links on those sites are still often valuable. We'll touch briefly on that in the following sections.

The key is to evaluate the site you want a link from and ensure it is relevant, well-maintained, and not filled with spammy, ad-driven content. With that, let's dive deeper into each link-building method.

CREATING COMPELLING BLOG POSTS ON YOUR OWN WEBSITE

We talked about creating content above, but when thinking about link building, here are a few thoughts to review:

- Identify your target audience: Before you start writing, it's essential to identify your target audience and understand their needs and interests. This will help you create content that resonates with them and other websites in your niche. Study those sites and what kind of content they create and post.
- Choose a relevant and timely topic: To create a compelling blog post, it's essential to choose an appropriate and timely topic. This could be a new book or another project you are working on, an event or news item related to the field you write in, or a trend or issue that interests your readers.
- Use a clear and compelling title that could work well as anchor text on another site: The title of your blog post is the first thing that readers will see, but it can also provide an easy path for another site to link to yours if it is relevant, brief, and catchy.
- Use images and other media to enhance the content: these will often entice another site to link to yours and your content.

Remember, your content can, and hopefully will, earn links to your website for you. The better your content, the easier it will be to earn those links.

GUEST BLOGGING FOR AUTHORS

Guest blogging is a strategy that involves writing blog posts for other websites related to yours. As stated above, you give a website owner a post or article to place on their blog (that you write for them), and they link to your site as part of the exchange. As an author, guest blogging can be a powerful way to reach a wider audience, build your reputation, and promote your books. Here are a few strategies for guest blogging as an author:

1. Identify relevant websites: To get the most out of your guest blogging efforts, it's crucial to identify websites pertinent to your genre and style and have an audience interested in your books and other writing. These websites often belong to other authors or are sites about books. They also include author interview sites, book review sites, and more.

2. Write valuable and informative posts: When writing your guest blog posts, it's essential to focus on creating content that addresses the needs and interests of the target website's audience, just like you do on your own site. This could be a behind-the-scenes look at your writing process, a discussion of the themes and ideas explored in your books, or insights and tips related to the topics you write about. Be careful about going too in-depth about your writing process: as we discussed related to your site, those posts will interest other authors more than they will readers. The goal is not only to earn a link to your site but to introduce readers of the other blog to you and what you do and hopefully turn them into your fans.

3. Include a bio and a link to your website: Most websites that accept guest blog posts will allow you to include a short bio and a link to your website at the end of your post. This is a second opportunity to promote your books and other writing and drive traffic to your website. Remember, the first should be to link to relevant content you have created on your website.

4. Engage with the website's audience: Comment on other blog posts and engage with the website's audience. This enables you to build relationships and establish yourself as a friendly fan and authority on the website topic.

A note here: there used to be a link-building method called "comment link building." Not only is this no longer effective, but it is also often marked as Spam by site owners. This means it can actually hurt your website ranking rather than help. Don't engage in it or try it as an author. It's both time-consuming and ineffective.

Guest blogging can also be fun, and I recommend that you allow others to guest post on your blog as well. You can even exchange guest posts, but like other marketing methods like email swaps, be sure to stay in your lane: only allow guest posts in your genre and on topics that your readers will be interested in.

Including a guest post about a steamy romance book on your mystery website will not work for your readers or another author. In fact, it might make some of them angry. Please don't risk it, and don't put your mystery posts on their steamy romance blog, either. It's not worth the risk.

But of the methods we will discuss here, guest blogging is one of the best and most effective ways to improve off-page SEO.

Now let's look at some less common link-building methods for authors.

NINE

UNCOMMON LINK BUILDING METHODS FOR AUTHORS

While guest posting is perhaps the most popular link-building strategy for authors, there are others as well. They are less common because they take more time and are more specialized.

There are two pieces of good news here: the first is that you do not have to use these methods at all. While they work well, they are not essential for most authors.

The second bit of good news is that if you take on these methods, you won't have a lot of competition out there. Few authors are engaged in them, so you might earn a wealth of links as a result.

Let's look at both of these methods and how they work for authors.

BROKEN LINK BUILDING FOR AUTHORS

Broken link building is a strategy that involves identifying broken links on other websites and offering to replace them with a link to a relevant and high-quality page on your own website. This can work, but a warning here: it is time-consuming and can be quite the rabbit hole. Also, many web owners receive spammy offers to regularly fix broken links on their sites. So, you should expect your offer to be rejected often.

However, staying on sites in your lane and having a respectful approach can be effective and has worked for some authors. Here are a few broken link-building methods authors can consider.

1. Check only relevant websites: Before you even identify broken links on other websites, it's important to determine whether the website is relevant to you and your readers. Again, please don't put your links in places where they are not helpful or on sites outside of your genre and general topic areas.
2. Use a broken link checker tool: There are several tools available that can help you identify broken links on other websites. Some popular options include Check My Links and Dead Link Checker.
3. Offer a replacement link: Once you have identified a broken link and a relevant website, you can offer to replace the broken link with a link to an appropriate and high-quality post or page on your own website. This could be a book page, a blog post, or another page that provides value to the website's audience. Ensure the link you offer fits the existing anchor text or can be easily modified to match your content. Offer anchor text with the link that shows you understand the scope and purpose of the article where the broken link exists. Be sure your link adds value to the topic as well.
4. Follow up: After offering to replace the broken link, it's essential to follow up with the website owner to ensure that your link has been added. You can also consider offering additional resources or assistance to the website

owner as a way to build a relationship and establish yourself as a helpful resource, including guest posting.

It's important to remember that the key to successful broken link building is to offer valuable and relevant content that addresses the needs and interests of the website's audience. Otherwise, the easiest solution for a link builder is to simply delete the broken link without replacing it.

You're asking for both the site owner's time and attention. Be sure your offer reflects your respect for that.

On a side note, I don't do a lot of broken link-building unless I spot something when researching a site for guest posting opportunities. It's too time-consuming for me, but it may work for you and your SEO strategy.

RESOURCE PAGE LINK BUILDING FOR AUTHORS

Resource page link building is a strategy that involves identifying resource pages on other websites relevant to your website and topics and offering to include a link to your website on those pages. Resource page link building can be a powerful way to build valuable backlinks to your website and improve its visibility and ranking in the search results.

The key to this method is that you also need to have a resource page or pages of your own. It would be best to have posts or pages that can serve as resources. Here are a few ways to get your link on resource pages as an author:

1. Identify relevant resource pages: Identify websites that have relevant resource pages. For some genres and authors, these pages either do not exist or are hard to find. If this method is irrelevant to your niche, don't force it.

2. Offer a valuable resource: Once you have identified a relevant resource page, you can offer to include a link to a valuable resource on your own website. This could be a book page, a blog post, or another page. Does your book offer information the site visitors would be interested in? Do you have a relevant blog post, or can you create one? Make sure your resource is a worthwhile one before you ask.

3. Follow-up: As with broken links, you can also consider offering additional resources or assistance to the website owner, like a guest post. Resource pages are often a great way to establish a relationship with a website and their audience.

Remember, as with guest posting, the key to successful resource page link building is to offer valuable and relevant content that addresses the needs and interests of the website's audience, not just yours. This can also be time-consuming, but it can create some valuable traffic and engagement for your website while improving overall site SEO and search rankings.

Next, let's take a look at social media and reviews.

TEN

SOCIAL MEDIA, REVIEWS, AND SEO

Social media, website, and book reviews can boost your SEO and your website's authority. How do they relate to SEO?

Well, let's take a look.

GENERATING SOCIAL MEDIA SHARES

What do you do with this content and those guest posts you have written? Share them on social media platforms. While search engines used to tell us these platforms do not matter to SEO, they have since revised that position. It does not matter as much as other links but it can make a difference.

While we will not go into social media strategy here (a different book and one I will not be likely to write), the point is that a backlink from your bio on social media links to your content that others will want to share; it all helps.

Also, social media can be a great way to expose your content to website owners who might want to link to it on their own websites and in their posts. Social media and social shares do matter to link building. Make it easy for your readers to share your content, share any guest posts you create on other sites with your audience, and keep up with the forever-changing trends.

NOTE: I will never say you must be on social media. There are plenty of writers who are not. So, if you hate it, you don't have to make it a part of your overall strategy. But it can be helpful for link-building, book sales, and other goals you may want to pursue. But it can also be time-consuming and depressing, so approach it cautiously.

GAINING MORE FOLLOWERS ON SOCIAL MEDIA

You can gain followers through guest posting, backlinks, and other methods using social media. If you are going to be present on social media, you might as well use it effectively. There are entire books and courses on this topic, but here are a few general guidelines:

1. Identify your target audience: Notice how I keep saying this repeatedly. Knowing your audience is essential for your blog, website, and all your marketing efforts, including social media.
2. Use relevant hashtags: Hashtags are a great way to connect with a broader audience and increase the visibility of your content. By using relevant hashtags related to your books and other writing, you can reach more people interested in your work. There are hashtag generators and research tools for nearly every social platform out there, so find the ones that work for you.
3. Engage with your followers: By responding to comments and messages, liking and commenting on other user's posts, and following them, you can build relationships, which is really what social media is all about. Don't just

be a loud sales voice in this space. It will not work and may do more harm than good.

4. Share valuable and engaging content: Your content. Guest posts. Other people's content. Thoughtful posts with no links. Social media content creation is its own topic, but it does share similarities with website content creation.

Gaining followers on social networks is good, most of the time. But again, you do not have to do it, and plenty of writers do not. But it can be an effective way to spread your content and even build links. But the most critical word in social media is social: this is about relationships, which is what your website can help you build as well.

One last tip on social media.

PRO TIP: NEVER PAY FOR SOCIAL MEDIA FOLLOWERS

There are several reasons why you should never pay for social media followers:

1. Fake followers: Many companies that sell social media followers use fake accounts or bots to inflate their numbers. These fake followers do not engage with your content and can actually harm your credibility and reputation.
2. Violation of social media terms of service: Most social media platforms have terms of service that prohibit the use of fake accounts or bots. By purchasing followers, you violate these terms and risk your account being suspended or banned.
3. Lack of engagement: Even if you manage to get real followers by paying for them, they are unlikely to engage

with your content. Many followers with very little actual engagement hurt your credibility and reputation.

4. Buying followers is a waste of money, as they do not bring any real value to your social media presence. Investing your time and resources into creating valuable and engaging content and building a genuine following through organic means is better.

This is like paying for reviews: it is just bad business. Please don't do it. Speaking of reviews…

REVIEWS

There are two aspects of reviews for authors, and both can help with off-page SEO. The first is website or business reviews, and the second is book reviews. We'll take a quick look at both without going too far down that rabbit hole:

EARNING POSITIVE WEBSITE REVIEWS AND MENTIONS

You might get good reviews and mentions if you offer author services or have a great website. There are blogs that I read and share regularly. It would be best if you had those too, but a part of your strategy with your website should be to establish yourself as an expert or resource.

This relates to good content, guest posting, and sharing your content far and wide. It also helps to share others' content because they are likelier to share yours. Remember, this is something earned, not that you ask for. Let reviews happen organically.

GETTING MORE BOOK REVIEWS

As an author, getting more reviews can be a powerful way to promote your books, build your reputation, and reach a wider audience. It's good for SEO, too. We won't go in-depth on this topic either, but it is worth mentioning as a part of your overall SEO strategy. Here are a few techniques for authors to get more reviews:

1. Ask your readers: One of the simplest and most effective ways to get more reviews is to simply ask your readers to leave one. You can do this by including a call to action in your book or on your website and sending your readers a personalized email.
2. Offer incentives: To encourage more readers to leave reviews, you can offer incentives such as a free book, a discount on future purchases, or exclusive content to a review team.
3. Participate in review swaps: Review swaps involve agreeing to review another author's book in exchange for them reviewing your book. Be careful with this: you must purchase each other's books to leave reviews on Amazon so you have a verified purchase. Otherwise, these are technically a violation of Amazon's terms of service. This can get you in real trouble, so if you do this, be sure to do it right. (More on that in a moment).
4. Use review sites: There are many websites and platforms that allow readers to leave reviews, such as Goodreads, Amazon, and Barnes & Noble. By encouraging your readers to leave reviews on these sites, you can reach a wider audience and get more visibility for your books.

Before we go any further, let's talk briefly about review swaps.

PROS AND CONS OF REVIEW SWAPS

Review swaps are a strategy that involves agreeing to review another author's book in exchange for them reviewing your book. Here are some of the pros and cons of review swaps for authors:

Pros:

- Build relationships: Review swaps can be a great way to build relationships with other authors in your genre or niche. This can help you connect with other professionals, learn from their experiences, and potentially collaborate on future projects.
- Get more reviews: By participating in review swaps, you can get more reviews for your books, which is almost never bad.
- Increase your reach: By reviewing other authors' books and having them review your books, you can reach their audience, and they can reach yours. This can have enormous benefits for each of you.

Cons:

- Time-consuming: Review swaps can be time-consuming, as you need to read and review other authors' books in addition to writing your own. DO NOT ever leave a review of an author's work you have not read. It can damage your reputation with readers if you do. Be sure you like the book before leaving any kind of review or rating.
- Risk of biased reviews: There is a risk that review swaps could lead to biased reviews, as authors may feel obligated to give a positive review in exchange for a review of their own book, even if they don't like yours.

Or if they give you a good review, you may feel you have to give one back.

- Not all authors are a good fit: Review swaps may not be effective if you cannot find authors whose books are a good fit for your audience. Remember, stay in your lane. Review books in your genre that would also interest your readers.

Review swaps can be good, but they can also be dangerous. Buy the other author's book. Avoid violations of terms and conditions, and never review a book without actually reading it. Don't ask anyone else to do so for your books, either.

WHY YOU SHOULD NEVER PAY FOR REVIEWS

Never, ever pay for book reviews, with very few exceptions:

- Ethical concerns: Some people may view paying for book reviews as a form of bribery since it could potentially influence the content of the review.
- Inauthenticity: When reviews are paid for, they may not accurately reflect the book's quality. This can mislead readers who rely on reviews to make informed purchasing decisions.
- Unreliability: Paid reviews may not be as reliable as reviews that are freely given. This is because the reviewer may not have the same level of motivation to provide an honest and thorough review if they are being compensated.
- Legal issues: In some cases, paying for reviews may be against the terms of service of certain review platforms or websites.

Some professional review sites coordinate reviews and offer review packages (but are honest), or like Kirkus, are considered valuable enough to pay for. Those cases are acceptable but be careful. Be sure you are paying for the company to coordinate reviews, not pay the reviewer themselves. Check out their reputation, and ensure reviews are honest and unbiased.

CONCLUSION

That's it for off-page optimization. Some of these topics could be books of their own, and some of them are. There are many resources out there about link building, guest posting, and more. For authors, please keep it simple and employ these techniques as part of an overall strategy. We'll talk about that toward the end of this book, but for now, we'll move on to measuring and analytics. How do you know if SEO is working? Let's take a look.

ELEVEN

ANALYZING YOUR WEBSITE TRAFFIC

I n this chapter, we will discuss how to measure and track the success of your SEO efforts. First, you need to establish some goals and standards for yourself. This is a part of your overall SEO Strategy.

It is essential to look at where your website traffic is coming from, whether web visitors are responding to your calls to action, and how changes to your website and SEO can influence those outcomes. Let's get started with setting goals and standards.

KEY PERFORMANCE INDICATORS (KPIS)

To track the success of your SEO efforts, it's essential to identify key performance indicators (KPIs) that will help you measure progress and identify areas for improvement. Some common KPIs for SEO include:

- **Organic traffic:** This refers to the number of visitors who come to your website from search engine results pages (SERPs), referral traffic, and even social media.

- **Search engine rankings:** This is the position your website ranks for in specific keyword searches.
- Paid Traffic refers to traffic that comes to your website through ads you have placed on other sites, including social media platforms.
- **Conversion rate:** The percentage of visitors who take a desired action on your website (such as signing up for a newsletter or purchasing a book or membership) is an important KPI to track.
- **Bounce rate** refers to the percentage of visitors leaving your website after viewing only one page. A high bounce rate can indicate that your website is not meeting the needs of your visitors.

TOOLS FOR TRACKING AND ANALYZING WEBSITE TRAFFIC AND RANKINGS

There are several tools available that can help you track and analyze your website's traffic and rankings. Some popular options include Google Analytics, SEMrush, and Moz. These tools can provide detailed information about your website's performance and insights into the keywords driving traffic to your site. I have a favorite, though, and we will look at that in more detail later in the book. It's called SEO Crawl.

First, let's look at defining and measuring organic website traffic.

WHAT IS ORGANIC WEBSITE TRAFFIC?

Organic website traffic refers to the visitors who come to your website through search engines, as opposed to paid advertising or other non-organic means. Here are a few types of organic website traffic:

- **Direct traffic:** This traffic arrives at your website directly, typically by typing your URL into the address bar of a browser. This type of traffic can indicate brand (read author) awareness and reader loyalty.
- **Referral traffic:** Traffic that arrives at your website from other websites, typically through links. This can be a good indicator of the quality and reach of your content and the strength of your relationships with other websites and organizations.
- **Search engine traffic** arrives at your website from search engines, typically through unpaid search results. This can be a good indicator of the visibility and relevance of your website in search results.
- **Social media traffic** arrives at your website from social media platforms, typically through shared links. This can be a good indicator of the engagement and reach of your social media presence.

Understanding the different types of organic website traffic can help you better understand your audience and the effectiveness of your marketing efforts.

Remember, we said that social media traffic and links used to not matter to SEO, or supposedly so. But you will likely see that much of your web traffic will come to your site via social media.

It's organic when it comes from posts you did not "boost" or from regular social media content, not from ads. That is paid traffic and a different topic altogether.

ANALYZING ORGANIC TRAFFIC

There are several tools available for tracking organic website traffic. Here are three examples:

- **Google Analytics:** This is a free, web-based analytics tool that provides detailed information about website traffic, including the number of visitors, the pages they visit, and how long they stay on the site. You'll need to install a tracking code on your website to use Google Analytics.
- **SEMrush:** This paid tool provides insights into organic traffic, keyword rankings, and other metrics related to search engine optimization (SEO). SEMrush uses data from various sources, including Google, to provide a comprehensive view of your website's performance.
- **Moz:** This is a suite of SEO tools with a feature for tracking organic traffic. In addition to traffic data, Moz also provides insights on keyword rankings, backlinks, and other SEO metrics.

All these tools work by collecting data from various sources and presenting it in a user-friendly interface, allowing you to track and analyze your website's organic traffic over time. As we have seen already, they do other things as well, but for this section, our focus is on traffic analysis.

WHAT IS REFERRAL TRAFFIC?

Referral website traffic refers to the visitors who arrive at your website from other websites, typically through links. These links can be in the form of text, banners, buttons, or different types of hyperlinks.

Referral traffic is a good indicator of the reach and quality of your website's content. If other websites link to your site, it may be because they find your content valuable or relevant to their audience. This can help increase your visibility and credibility.

Referral traffic can also indicate the strength of your relationships with other websites and organizations. You'll likely see more referral traffic from their sites if you have a strong network of partners or affiliates.

Overall, referral website traffic can be an essential source of web visitors. Remember, this is only considered organic if it happens naturally. This can be through guest posts and backlink building, but referral traffic is not regarded as organic if it comes through ads you have placed on another site.

We use the same tools to analyze referral traffic as we do to analyze organic traffic.

ANALYZING REFERRAL TRAFFIC

What can you learn from looking at referral traffic? You can understand what guest posts or articles perform best, which pages influence web visitors most, and more.

THE SOURCES OF YOUR REFERRAL TRAFFIC

By looking at the websites that are sending traffic to your site, you can better understand the reach and quality of your content. You can also identify specific websites or organizations driving significant traffic to your site.

1. The types of content that are most popular: By analyzing the specific pages or posts that are receiving the most referral traffic, you can get a sense of what resonates with your audience. This can help you identify opportunities to create similar or related content in the future.
2. The performance of your marketing efforts: If you're working with affiliates or partners to promote your website, analyzing referral traffic can help you understand the effectiveness of those efforts. You can see

which websites or campaigns drive the most traffic and adjust your strategy accordingly.

3. Growth opportunities: By looking at the websites that are sending traffic to your site, you may identify opportunities for collaboration or partnerships that could help you grow your traffic further. You may also be able to identify areas where your content is underperforming and make improvements or stop creating those kinds of posts altogether.

Overall, analyzing referral traffic can provide valuable insights into the performance and reach of your website. But it also shows you where to focus your efforts.

For example, if you are getting web traffic from specific podcasts or websites, perhaps you can increase your partnership with them or even engage in paid ads on those sites. If you are posting regularly on a site and seeing no traffic from them at all, that can help you decide how much effort to put into maintaining that relationship.

WHERE IS REFERRAL TRAFFIC GOING?

Referral traffic is fantastic, but seeing where it is going is essential. What pages and posts are getting attention? Especially if these are organic links, this is vital to your overall strategy. It can also show you what keywords you are ranking for.

Referral links also reveal what anchor text leads people to your website. With a link in your bio, this will often be your name or "visit my website," or even a "naked URL" with your website link spelled out.

But if you are getting links from anchor text like "mystery author" or "historical romance author" or the title of a blog post, that is even better. It shows that those keywords also matter to other bloggers and website owners.

Getting a lot of referral traffic tells you one of two things: either you are doing a great job guest posting and link building, or you are creating great content that is earning organic links. You may even be experiencing both, which is even better. It shows you have a good overall SEO strategy, good content and that your efforts are paying off.

A lot of relevant referral traffic leads to the next type of traffic.

SEARCH ENGINE TRAFFIC

Search engine traffic is a result of one thing: your rankings. This means you are ranking on the first page of Google for at least some keywords. Search engine traffic reports will show what keywords you are ranking for.

Those keywords are likely linking to certain focused pages or posts. Here are some tips for analyzing search engine traffic.

- Use tools like Google Analytics, MOZ, SEM Rush, or SEO Crawl to look at the number of visitors that come to your site through search, the pages they visit, and how long they stay on the site. It also provides data on the keywords that drive traffic.
- Identify your top-performing pages: You can identify the pages receiving the most traffic through user searches. These pages may be good candidates for further optimization or promotion.
- Analyzing search keywords reveals what users are searching for that drives traffic to your website and helps you understand what topics or terms are most relevant to those searchers. It also shows if those keywords result

in searchers taking the desired action on your website (purchases or lead generation)

In other words, look at what keywords and categories you rank well for and create more related content with similar keywords and formats.

For example, suppose you rank well for a video on serial killer motives you created and hosted on your website. In that case, you can create written content around that theme, a long-form article, and even more articles that address individual motives and their psychology.

More readers will come to your site for your content, and may turn into leads, fans, and buyers, which is your ultimate goal.

This is only one of the reasons keeping things relevant is so important. Your post on great BBQ recipes may bring traffic, but are those book buyers also? If not, you are wasting time and energy, even though your site might rank well for odd keywords.

This is not to discount ranking in various keywords, but it is a caution that relevance, as I have stated before, is vital to SEO success.

SOCIAL MEDIA TRAFFIC

Remember how we said social media is important to SEO? It is, and it is also key to getting more social media traffic. By analyzing social media traffic to your website, you can learn several things, including:

1. The social media platforms that drive the most traffic to your website: You can identify which social media platforms work best for you. This can help you

understand where to focus your efforts for maximum impact.

2. The types of content that are most popular on social media: By analyzing the specific pages or posts receiving the most social media traffic, you can get a sense of what types of content resonate with your audience. This can help you identify opportunities to create similar or related content in the future.

3. Performance: Analyzing social media traffic can help you understand the effectiveness of your social media marketing efforts. You can see which posts or campaigns drive the most traffic and adjust your strategy accordingly, including your ad strategy.

4. Opportunities: You may also identify opportunities for collaboration or partnerships to help you grow your traffic further and identify areas where your content is underperforming.

Analyzing social media traffic can provide valuable insights into your overall social media strategy. You can identify what networks perform best for you, what content your audience resonates with, what hashtags and topics perform best, and more. You can take this data and use it to improve.

PAID TRAFFIC

Many authors run ads on social media and other platforms. While often these ads direct readers to Amazon or other book retailers, if you are engaged in ads for lead generation or to build direct sales, those visitors may come directly to your website. But how do you know if ads are working?

You analyze them just like you did with all the other traffic types listed above. We use the same tools, but when you look at a specific website you have run ads on or a page where your

Facebook or other social media ads lead, the results will give you a lot of insight.

The main one is conversion. Ads most often lead to a landing page, and as we stated, the purpose of those pages is to get the visitor to do one thing: purchase something or join your email list.

We'll talk about conversion rates shortly and how to calculate them, but the most important thing you will look at in relation to landing pages is what percentage of people who land on your page take the action you want them to. The higher that percentage, the better.

Of course, there are things you can do to your landing pages to improve those conversions, and that is an entirely different book, but they include the correct keywords (on the page and in your ads) and strong calls to action.

The key is understanding that the more search and referral traffic you get from specific keywords, the more search engines associate your site with those areas of expertise or topics. This helps increase your rankings, and that first page of Google before you scroll or page forward is the place to be.

Now that we've looked at the four primary website traffic sources, let's take a moment to understand conversions.

UNDERSTANDING CONVERSION RATES ON AUTHOR WEBSITES

Conversion rates measure how effective your website is at achieving a specific goal, such as making a sale or generating a lead. To determine the conversion rate on an author's website, you'll need to set up a goal in your website analytics tool and track the number of conversions (i.e., goal completions) over a specific period.

As we stated before, some author goals include:

- Lead generation, like people joining your email list or showing interest in your books.
- Direct book sales: selling books from your website rather than an online retailer, where you keep a larger percentage of the profits.
- Build awareness of upcoming books and campaigns or events you may participate in.

To calculate the conversion rate, divide the number of conversions by the number of visitors to your website and multiply by 100. For example, if you had 100 visitors to your website and 10 of them completed a goal (such as purchasing a book), your conversion rate would be 10%.

It's a good idea to track your conversion rate over time to understand how it's changing and identify any trends or patterns. You can also compare your conversion rate to key benchmarks to see how your website performs compared to other authors or book retailers.

To improve your conversion rate, you may want to consider testing different elements of your website, such as the layout, design, or calls to action, to see what works best. You can also analyze the behavior of visitors who convert versus those who don't to identify potential areas for improvement.

For example, if you have a landing page for people to sign up for your newsletter and get a free lead magnet, your conversion rate should be pretty high. If it is not, you may want to look at the landing page itself, the call to action, the form and how it is formatted, and more. A form that is not mobile-friendly or asks for too much information will likely have a lower conversion rate.

BOUNCE RATE AND HOW TO DECREASE IT

A negative metric we look at is the bounce rate. This is not as bad as it sounds sometimes, and for author sites, it is sometimes higher than other sites. The reason is that people often visit your site to read a single blog post or sign up for your newsletter, and there is nowhere else for them to go (although setting up a redirect after they sign up for your newsletter can reduce this "bounce rate.")

Bounce rate measures the percentage of visitors to your website who leave after viewing only one page. A high bounce rate can indicate that visitors aren't finding what they're looking for on your website, your website isn't engaging enough to keep them there, or they are not responding to your call to action by making a purchase or subscribing to your newsletter. Here are a few strategies you can use to decrease the bounce rate on your author website:

- Ensure your website is easy to navigate: A confusing or poorly designed website can lead to a high bounce rate, as visitors may have difficulty finding what they're looking for. Make sure your menu is visible and simple, and your pages include clear calls to action to help visitors find what they're looking for and encourage them to explore your website further.
- Optimize your website for mobile: More and more people are accessing the web from their smartphones, so it's essential to ensure your website is optimized for mobile. A website that's difficult to use on a smartphone can lead to a high bounce rate, as visitors may leave if they can't easily access your content.
- Use internal linking: Internal linking is the process of linking to other pages on your website from within your

content. This can help visitors explore your website further by reading multiple articles on a similar topic.

- Use engaging, high-quality content: High-quality, engaging content can help keep visitors on your website longer, which can help decrease the bounce rate. Make sure your content is well-written, informative, and relevant.

Decreasing the bounce rate on your author website is about improving the overall user experience for your visitors. It's important to regularly analyze and optimize your website to ensure that it meets your audience's needs. It is easy to let pages and posts get out of date, and your web visitors will notice. So, take the time to make updates regularly.

AVOIDING SPAMMY LINKS TO YOUR SITE

Now that we have reached the downside of SEO, we must go to the dark side and discuss spammy links. The more content you produce and the more popular it is, the more likely you will get some spammy or questionable sites that link to your content. Sometimes, you may even link build using some of these sites without realizing they are classified as spam.

These can include gambling sites, porn sites, and sites that are part of private blog networks (PBN) set up to make money from ads. It can also include fake news sites, like the infamous washingtonpost.co and denvergazette.com (not an actual publication).

To find out, you should do a link audit at least annually. This means taking tools like MOZ and SEM Rush and looking at your backlink profile. Look for questionable sites, most with low domain authority or trustworthiness. This will show you the following:

- What sites are linking to yours?
- What keywords do they use in the anchor text linking to your site?
- What pages they are linking to.
- What are your top pages and keywords?
- The quality of the sites linking to yours

When you see this, there are a few things you can do about it. Here are some of the ones you can use to avoid those links in the first place.

1. Use the "rel=nofollow" attribute: You can use the "rel=nofollow" attribute to tell search engines not to follow links to your website when determining your ranking. This can be useful if you have links you don't want to pass any SEO value (or devalue) to your website.
2. Monitor your link profile: It's a good idea to regularly monitor your link profile to identify any low-quality or spammy links pointing to your website. This can help you identify and address potential issues before they become a problem.
3. Disavow spammy links: If you have many spammy links that you can't remove or nofollow, you may want to consider disavowing those links. Disavowing links is a process of telling search engines to ignore certain links when determining your ranking. However, this can be a complex and time-consuming process.
4. Use the "nofollow" tag: If you can't remove or disavow a link, you can ask the site owner to use the "nofollow" tag to tell search engines not to follow the link or ignore the link's content. This can help prevent the link from influencing your ranking.

Before you go to the trouble of disavowing links, contact the site owners, and ask for your links to be removed or marked "nofollow." But it's more important to determine whether the link will actually damage your website's reputation or authority. In most cases, the impact will be small or not even noticeable.

The best way to combat these spammy links is to get more legitimate, good ones. These will effectively "bury" the bad ones, and that is the best way to minimize their impact. But if you must disavow links, here are some pros and cons.

PROS AND CONS DISAVOWING LINKS

As we stated, disavowing links is a process of telling search engines to ignore certain links pointing to your website when determining your website's ranking in search results. This is typically done when you have many low-quality or spammy links pointing to your website, which could potentially harm your ranking. Note this says, "large number." If you only have a few spammy links, this effort is not likely worth it.

To disavow links, you'll need to create a file that lists the links you want to disavow and submit it to the search engines through their webmaster tools or other channels. The search engines will then evaluate your request and most often ignore those links when evaluating your website's ranking.

It's important to note that disavowing links is a last resort and should only be done after other efforts to remove the links have been unsuccessful. Disavowing links can be a time-consuming and complex process. It's also hard to verify: tools like MOZ and SEM Rush will often still show those links pointing to your site because they cannot "see" if Google or other search engines ignore them.

If you're considering disavowing links to your website, take the other steps mentioned above, and always try contacting the site owner first.

If these efforts are unsuccessful or you have many low-quality links that you can't remove or noindex, you may want to consider disavowing them. However, at this point, you might want to hire someone to do this for you to save you both time and frustration.

TOOL TIP: SEOCRAWL

SEOCrawl is a website analytics and SEO tool that helps users understand and improve the performance of their websites. It's a tool I use because it is easy, and I share it with another author so we can track several sites. Like other tools, here are a few ways you can use SEOCrawl for website analytics:

1. Keyword tracking: SEOCrawl allows you to track your website's performance for specific keywords, including your ranking in search results and the number of searches for those keywords. This can help you understand how well your website performs for particular keywords and identify opportunities for improvement.
2. On-page SEO analysis: SEOCrawl provides a detailed analysis of your website's on-page SEO, including the presence and use of keywords, the structure of your URLs, and the use of header tags. This can help you identify issues with your on-page SEO and improve your visibility in search results.
3. Backlink analysis: SEOCrawl provides information on the backlinks pointing to your website, including the quality and quantity of those links. This can help you understand the strength of your website's link profile

and identify opportunities for building high-quality backlinks.

4. Technical SEO analysis: SEOCrawl analyzes various technical aspects of your website, including the speed of your pages, the use of mobile-friendly design, and the presence of broken links. This can help you identify technical issues that may negatively impact your website's performance and make improvements to increase your visibility in search results.

SEOCrawl combines the power of several tools to make analysis faster, more efficient, and easier if you are not an SEO expert who is used to diving into Google's tools in depth. You can even connect Google tools so that you can look at that data all in one place as well.

By regularly tracking and analyzing your website's performance, looking at your backlink profile, and making revisions and updates, you can identify areas for improvement and adjust your SEO strategy as needed. The next chapter will look at some other outcomes authors want from their websites and how you can make them work for you.

TWELVE
LEAD GENERATION AND DIRECT SALES

As we have discussed, two of the most common things authors do with their websites are lead generation and direct sales to readers. The same techniques that apply to direct sales also apply to third-party selling - to an extent.

Let's take a quick look at these in detail.

LEAD GENERATION

Lead generation attracts and converts potential customers or clients into leads, individuals who have expressed interest in your books or other merchandise. Lead generation can be important for authors in building an audience and promoting your books. The goal is usually to get that person to sign up for your newsletter, SMS messages, or website notifications. Here are a few strategies you can use for lead generation as an author:

- Build an email list using your website: An email list is a valuable asset for lead generation, as it allows you to stay in touch with your audience and promote your books directly to them. You can build an email list by offering incentives such as free chapters or discounts on your books as an incentive for readers to sign up.

- Utilize social media: Social media platforms can be a powerful tool for lead generation, allowing you to share information about your books and interact with potential readers. You can use social media to share updates, run promotions, engage with your audience, and get them to sign up for your email list.
- Ask readers to follow you on BookBub, Amazon, and other platforms like Goodreads. Join contests and giveaways that incentivize readers to follow you and other authors. This way, the reader gets notified whenever you have a new book release, a sale, and more.
- Use your books to gain email addresses and follows. Have links in the back of your books that lead to your email signup forms and your profile on those platforms where you want readers to follow you.
- Host events: Hosting events, such as book readings or workshops, can be a great way to generate leads and connect with your audience in person. You can promote these events through your website and social media channels and collect email addresses from attendees.

It's essential to be consistent and persistent in your lead generation efforts and to regularly analyze and optimize them to ensure you're getting the best results possible. Also, understand that every lead generation technique is not for every author. Some people hate social media or in-person events.

But everyone can use different methods to build your email list and keep in touch with readers. Here are some additional tips on building your email list.

BUILDING YOUR EMAIL LIST AS AN AUTHOR

There are entire books, courses, and debates about how to build your email list as an author. We won't go into all those here other than to say your website and overall SEO can play a role in your list building. Here are a few common tactics.

- Offer a freebie: One effective way to get people to sign up for your email list is to offer a freebie, such as the first book in your series for free (if you have a series) or a related novella or short story. This can be a good incentive, but you can expect to get those who come for the free book and then unsubscribe immediately. There are strategies to deal with this, and you can find other resources that outline those techniques.
- Use a sign-up form: Make it easy for people to sign up for your email list by including a sign-up form on your website and linking to it from your social media profiles. It is even better if you have signup landing pages dedicated to the single purpose of gaining email subscribers.
- You can also include a link to a sign-up form in the back matter of your book to encourage readers to join your email list. This is a good tactic, as they already know (and like) your work.
- Run a contest or giveaway: Contests and giveaways can be a great way to attract email subscribers. You can offer a prize related to your book, such as a signed copy or exclusive merchandise, and draw a random winner. Like freebies, you can and should expect a certain percentage of people to sign up for the giveaway and unsubscribe when it is over. This is why a robust welcome sequence to your email list is really important.
- Partner with other authors or organizations: Partnering with other authors or organizations can be an excellent

way to expand your email list. You can cross-promote each other's email lists or run a joint giveaway to attract new subscribers. You can even do email swaps, but remember, as we discussed before: stay in your lane and your genre. Don't mix things up. You'll get the wrong subscribers, hurting you in the long run.

- Use social media: Social media platforms, including paid ads, can be an excellent way to promote your email list and attract new subscribers. You can share updates about your email list, run promotions, and engage with your audience to encourage them to sign up.

There are all kinds of other tips related to your email list, including list maintenance and culling, and even encouraging people who are not interested in your content long-term to unsubscribe. This involves a welcome sequence and various automations, which all have value. But since they don't bear directly on SEO, other than their potential impact on the number and type of site visitors you receive, we won't go in-depth into them here.

NOTE: you do not have to have an email list, just like you do not have to have social media. It is a powerful tool, and if you don't have one, you will need to build a community and following in other ways. But as with social media, I would never say an author who does not email will not find success.

I will say that success may be more complex, but there are all kinds of business models out there, and it is important you choose the one that is right for you and your books.

Next, let's talk briefly about direct sales and how selling books and other merchandise directly on your site can impact your SEO and vice-versa.

DIRECT SALES AND SEO

One of the biggest reasons for a resurgence of SEO for authors is the rise of authors selling books and merchandise direct from their own websites. This includes audio, eBooks, and physical books, and while not a new strategy, it is gaining in popularity again.

In this case, conversions and landing pages are even more critical than ever. Because conversions equal sales, those sales are at the highest profit margin. Also, you can get more data from those sales than from Amazon or any other retailer. This is part of an author strategy called "wider than wide."

While this method includes other strategies like Kickstarter and other platforms, for this discussion, we will focus on your website and how direct sales impacts SEO and vice versa.

First, direct sales mean you will have more pages on your website, depending on how you set things up. If you stick with WordPress as your base, you can treat each product as a "post" or a "page." Each approach has pros and cons, but the SEO approach remains the same.

Of course, you will also want to rank for more book-specific keywords. And if you offer your books on other platforms (you should, as a wider-than-wide strategy), you may have trouble outranking those sites. The key is to educate your readers through your newsletter and social media that your website is the cheapest and best place to purchase your books.

Second, this also impacts your ad strategy. You should direct people to your website through your calls to action on Facebook and other ad platforms and add your own website to your Universal Book Links.

All of this helps you rank better for book titles and keywords related to those titles. Don't forget your series names as keywords as well. Building direct sales can take time, but probably less time than you think.

Remember, we said way back at the beginning of this book that SEO takes about 90 days to produce real results, but that is also a slope that can be impacted by how good your website is already, what your SEO skills and efforts are, and the ads you support your efforts with.

Here are a few additional strategies you can use to generate book sales directly from your author website:

- Make it easy to purchase your books: Make it easy for visitors to buy your books by including clear calls to action and links to online retailers if readers want to purchase there rather than from your online store. Within your store, have an easy checkout process that offers as many options as possible.
- Offer multiple purchase options, such as print, audio, or digital versions of your book. The more options your reader has, the more likely they will purchase from you and your store.
- Offer exclusive content or incentives: You can incentivize sales by offering exclusive content within each book or other perks to visitors who purchase your book directly from your website. Offer swag with physical books where possible, bonus digital editions, series bundles, and the lowest prices anywhere. This can be an excellent way to encourage people to buy from you rather than a third-party retailer.
- Use social media to promote your online bookstore: Utilize social media to promote your website and drive traffic to your products. Share updates about your books, post sample chapters or excerpts, and engage with your audience. Don't forget to target your site and direct sales with your ad strategy.

- Run promotions or sales: Running promotions or sales can be a good way to generate book sales from your website. You can offer discounts, bundle your books with other products, or offer seasonal deals. Use various coupon codes so you know where your web traffic and purchases are coming from.
- Use email marketing: Email marketing can be a powerful tool for driving sales from your website. You can use your email list to promote your books, share updates, and run promotions to encourage purchases. As we have mentioned, building your email list is one of the best and most valuable things you can do as part of your overall marketing strategy, and it is good for SEO too.

If you sell directly to readers from your website, a good overall strategy with a broader set of keywords is essential to success. SEO plays a huge role and is more critical the more your site becomes a community and hub for your sales and lead generation.

THIRD-PARTY BOOK AND MERCHANDISE SALES

Setting up your website to sell books directly is a big project requiring some technical skills. There are things you can do to avoid having to be the technical service and customer service rep for your site, but it requires some knowledge.

Not that you shouldn't make the effort. Selling from your website can be profitable, but it works best if you have an extensive backlist, a fan base to work with, and some money to invest.

So many writers have links on their websites that point to third-party websites like Amazon and other book retailers. These work, but measuring how they work can be a little trickier.

In that case, a conversion is someone who clicked on the link to go to Amazon. You can't see (easily) if that person purchased your book or not.

However, everything we said about direct sales applies, with some exceptions. You can offer exclusive deals for email subscribers or those who follow certain links, but you may not know the outcome of those transactions.

However, you can still use your site to promote any sales or discounts you can offer on other retailers and can still direct readers to your work.

You'll still want a good email list and one you "take care of" by staying in touch with them and engaging with them.

THIRTEEN

ADVANCED SEO TECHNIQUES

This chapter will discuss advanced SEO techniques that can help you take your optimization efforts to the next level. These are not necessary for every author's website, and you don't have to do any of them.

However, they are good to be aware of. And a few, like optimizing for mobile use and knowing about Google Core Vitals, while not a must, are definitely advised. It pays for you to go through this section to see what applies to you and then go from there.

Check it out for yourself.

LOCAL SEO FOR AUTHORS WITH PHYSICAL STOREFRONTS OR EVENTS

Optimizing your website for local search is essential if you have a physical storefront or hold local events. Local SEO refers to optimizing a website for the specific location of the business or event. This can include optimizing for local keywords, such as the city or neighborhood name, and including your business's location and contact information on your website.

Local SEO is the process of optimizing your online presence to rank highly in local search results. As an author, local SEO can be an essential part of promoting your books and events to a local audience. Here are a few strategies you can use to improve your local SEO:

1. Claim your Google My Business listing: Google My Business is a free tool that allows you to manage your online presence across Google, including Google Maps and Google Search. By claiming and verifying your listing, you can improve your local SEO and make it easier for people to find your business online. Note here: you can use a P.O. Box if you do not have a physical location that is not your home. You may not want to publicize your home address unless you conduct business there.

2. Use local keywords: Include local keywords in your website's content and metadata to signal to search engines that your business is relevant to a specific location. For example, if you're an author in Chicago, you might include the keywords "author Chicago" in your website's content and metadata. A friend uses: "one of the bestselling authors in Idaho" in his local marketing.

3. Get listed in local directories: Local directories, such as Yelp or Yellow Pages (online, of course), can help improve your local SEO by providing additional links to your website. Ensure your business is listed in as many relevant local directories as possible.

4. Encourage customer reviews: Customer reviews can help improve your local SEO by providing additional content for search engines to index and by signaling to search engines that your business is relevant and trustworthy. Encourage your customers to leave reviews on your Google My Business listing and other review

sites. As an author, this can be an overall review of your work in general, any services you offer to fans and readers, or other businesses.

By following these strategies, you can improve your local SEO and make it easier for people in your local area to find your books and events and even increase their awareness of other local authors. It's important to be consistent and persistent in your local SEO efforts and to regularly analyze and optimize your approach to ensure you get the best results possible.

PRO TIP: CONNECT WITH YOUR LOCAL BOOKSTORES

Another best practice for increasing your local SEO: connect with your local bookstores. Not only can they carry your books and host events, but they can also make people aware of local authors in a new way.

NOTE: most of the time, this means your local, independent bookstore, although sometimes you can connect with Barnes and Noble or other large chains. Remember that bookstores have limited shelf space and stock books that sell, so be sure to send readers there to purchase your books. You are not doing the bookstore a favor by allowing them to stock your books. They are doing you a favor by carrying them.

Approach the bookstore owner with humility, and if they tell you no to stocking your book, understand they probably have a business-related reason to do so. Here are a few tips to follow when reaching out to connect with local bookstores:

1. Research local bookstores: Take some time to research the local bookstores in your area and get a sense of their selection and customer base. This will help you tailor

your approach and identify the stores most likely to be interested in carrying your book.

2. Reach out to store owners and managers: Contact the owners and managers of local bookstores directly to introduce yourself and your book. Be sure to highlight relevant details, such as your book's subject matter or target audience.

3. Offer to do a reading or signing: Many local bookstores are open to hosting events, such as book readings or signings, to promote local authors. Offer to do a reading or signing at the store to help promote your book and build relationships with the store's staff.

4. Participate in local events: Local events, such as book fairs or festivals, can be an excellent way to connect with local bookstores and other authors. Consider participating in these events and networking with store owners and managers to build relationships and promote your book.

5. Utilize social media: social media can be a powerful tool for connecting with local bookstores and promoting your book. Follow local bookstores on social media and engage with their content to build relationships and promote your book.

By following these tips, you can effectively connect with local bookstores and promote your book to a local audience. But again, remember that this is about engagement and relationships. Do not expect the local bookstore just automatically to say yes to you.

And if you have not engaged with them or other writers in your local community, you may want to start doing so sooner rather than later. You should be known for who you are and what you do in your area, even if that is not the primary market for your work.

MOBILE OPTIMIZATION FOR AUTHORS

As we said above, with the increasing use of mobile devices to access the internet, ensuring your website is optimized for mobile is important. Google and other search engines are prioritizing mobile responsiveness as well, and it's becoming more and more critical.

This includes ensuring that your website is responsive (meaning it adjusts to fit the size of the device it's being viewed on) and has a fast loading speed. You can use Google's Mobile-Friendly Test tool to check if your website is mobile-friendly. Here are some tips for making sure your site is mobile-friendly.

If some of the technical aspects of this section seem too challenging, you can always hire a developer to make small changes to ensure your site works well on any device.

Tips for a Mobile-Friendly Website

Here are some tips for optimizing your author website for mobile users:

1. Use a responsive design: As mentioned above, it ensures that your website adjusts automatically to fit the screen size of the device it's being viewed on. This is important for mobile users, as your website is easy to use and navigate on a small screen.
2. Simplify navigation: Mobile users have limited screen real estate, so keeping your navigation simple and easy to use is essential. Consider using a hamburger menu or other mobile-friendly navigation options to make it easy for users to find what they're looking for.
3. Optimize images: Large or poorly optimized images can slow down your website and make mobile use difficult. Ensure your images are optimized for the web and load quickly on mobile devices. Don't be tempted to use

large, high-resolution galleries and slide shows. Think simple but elegant when it comes to mobile.

4. Use large, easy-to-read text: Mobile users may have difficulty reading small or difficult-to-read text, so it's essential to use large, easy-to-read text on your website.

5. Avoid using pop-ups: Pop-ups can be annoying and difficult to close on mobile, leading to a high bounce rate. Consider using alternative methods like forms and buttons for capturing email addresses or promoting your books.

6. Simplify forms: Mobile users may have difficulty filling out long or complex forms, so keeping your forms as simple as possible is essential. Consider using a tool like Google Forms or the Forminator Pro plugin if you use WordPress to create mobile-friendly forms.

7. Use white space: White space can help make your website more visually appealing and easier to read on mobile devices. Use white space to separate different sections of your website, making it easier for users to focus on the content.

8. Use bullet points or numbered lists: Bullet points and numbered lists can help break up your content and make it easier to read on mobile devices.

9. Use mobile-friendly CTAs: Make sure your calls to action (CTAs) are easy to tap on mobile devices. Use large buttons or other mobile-friendly designs to make it easy for users to act.

Most searches are now done on mobile devices. As a result, Google has established Google Core Values to make sure sites are as mobile-friendly as possible.

Google periodically updates its mobile standards to ensure that websites are optimized for mobile devices and provide a good user experience. These updates can significantly impact the ranking of websites in Google's search results, as the company prefers websites that are both responsive and easy to navigate.

Here are a few examples of recent updates to Google's mobile standards and why they matter:

1. Mobile-first indexing: In 2019, Google introduced mobile-first indexing, which means that it now uses the mobile version of a website as the primary source for indexing and ranking. This update is crucial because it means that websites not optimized for mobile may be disadvantaged in search results.
2. Page speed: Google has long emphasized the importance of page speed in its mobile standards and has released several tools and guidelines to help websites improve their loading times. A slow-loading website can lead to a high bounce rate, negatively impacting your ranking in search results.
3. Pop-ups and interstitials: In 2017, Google updated its mobile standards to penalize websites that use pop-ups or interstitials that interfere with the user's ability to access content. Pop-ups and interstitials can be annoying and disruptive for users and negatively impact their experience.

By following Google's mobile standards, authors can improve their ranking in search results and provide a better user experience for their mobile users.

Consider that a lot of reading is done on mobile devices through apps like Kindle, Kobo, Nook, and Apple Books. If readers can find, purchase, and read your books on a single device, that is a win for you.

Google Core Web Vitals and Why They Matter

Google Core Web Vitals are a set of metrics that measure the quality of a user's experience on the web. These metrics focus on three key areas: loading speed, interactivity, and visual stability. Google has identified these areas as particularly important for providing a good user experience and has developed a set of metrics to help measure them.

Here are a few examples of Google Core Web Vitals and why they matter:

1. Largest Contentful Paint (LCP): LCP measures the time it takes for the main content of a webpage to load and become visible to the user. A slow LCP can lead to a poor user experience, as users may become frustrated if they have to wait too long for a webpage to load.
2. First Input Delay (FID): FID measures the time it takes for a webpage to become interactive, meaning that users can interact with it and input commands. A slow FID can lead to a poor user experience, as users may become frustrated if they have to wait too long for a webpage to become interactive.
3. Cumulative Layout Shift (CLS): CLS measures the stability of a webpage's layout as it loads. A high CLS can lead to a poor user experience, as users may become frustrated if the layout of a webpage shifts unexpectedly as it loads.

It's important for authors to be aware of these metrics and to make sure their website is meeting the standards set by Google to provide a good user experience and improve their ranking in search results. Again, if things get too technical for your abilities, don't be afraid to seek help from a pro.

But for the most part, you can do this by following a few simple steps with a good web host and web builder. Many will offer two versions of your website, a standard and an m.yourwebsitename.com version, to which phones and other devices are automatically directed.

Advanced techniques such as structured data and schema markup

Structured data is a way to annotate your website's content so that search engines can better understand the meaning and context of the information on your website. This can include adding tags to your website's HTML code to indicate the type of content (such as a product review or event listing) and to provide additional context (such as the date of an event or the price of a product).

ADDING STRUCTURED DATA

Structured data is a standardized format for providing information about a webpage to search engines. It allows search engines to understand the content of a webpage and provide more relevant and accurate results to users. Here are a few ways you can create structured data for your website:

- Use schema.org: Schema.org is a standardized vocabulary for describing the content of a webpage. You can use schema.org to mark up your website's content with specific tags that provide information about the page to search engines.
- Use Google's Structured Data Markup Helper: Google's Structured Data Markup Helper is a tool that allows you to add structured data to your website easily. The tool guides you through the process of marking up your webpage's content and generates the necessary code for you to add to your website.
- Use JSON-LD: JSON-LD (JavaScript Object Notation for Linking Data) is a standardized format for adding structured data to a webpage. You can use JSON-LD to

add structured data to your website by including it in a script tag in the head of your webpage.

Using these tools and techniques, you can add structured data to your website and help search engines understand the content of your pages, and you can do it yourself. Before you get started, it's important to carefully review the guidelines provided by schema.org and Google to ensure you're using the correct tags and formatting for your structured data to get the maximum benefit.

For most writers, this is an unnecessary step: but if you are selling directly from your website, you may want to engage in more advanced techniques to ensure your SEO is the best it can be. In addition to structured data, you can also add schema markup.

Schema Markup

Schema markup is a specific type of structured data used to provide additional context about the content on your website. By using schema markup, you can help search engines understand the relationships between different types of content on your website, which can improve the way your website appears in search results.

Schema markup is a standardized vocabulary for describing the content of a webpage. By adding schema markup to your website, you can help search engines understand the content of your pages and provide more relevant and accurate results to users. Here are the steps for adding schema markup to your website:

1. Determine what type of schema you want to use: There are many different types of schema, including product, event, recipe, and article schema. Determine the schema type most relevant to your website and the content you

want to mark up. For authors, this is most often product, event, and article.

2. Choose the specific properties you want to mark up: Each type of schema has a list of specific properties that you can mark up. Choose the properties most relevant to your content that you want to include in your schema markup.

3. Use the Google Structured Data Markup Helper or another tool to generate the schema markup code: Google's Structured Data Markup Helper is a tool that allows you to add schema markup to your website easily. Choose the type of schema you want to use and the specific properties you want to mark up, and the tool will generate the necessary code for you to add to your website.

4. Add the schema markup code to your website: Once you have it, you can include it in the head or body of your webpage. Make sure to test your schema markup using Google's Structured Data Testing Tool to ensure it is correctly implemented.

Again, before you get started, carefully review the guidelines provided by schema.org and Google. If this gets too in the weeds for you, consider hiring a pro to do this part of the process for you.

Example: Using DIVI to Add Structured Data and Schema Markup

DIVI is a popular WordPress page builder plugin that allows you to create and customize your website's layout and design easily. Here's how you can add structured data and schema markup to your website using DIVI:

1. Once you have followed the steps above to determine the type of structured data or schema you want to add, create the necessary code.
2. Add the schema markup code to your website: Once you have it, you can add it using the DIVI builder. Go to the page or post to which you want to add the schema markup, click on the "Add Code Module" button, and paste the schema markup code into the module.
3. Test your schema markup using Google's Structured Data Testing Tool: After adding the schema markup code to your website, just like if you do so with another builder other than DIVI, it is important to test it using Google's Structured Data Testing Tool to ensure that it is correctly implemented.

Following these steps, you can use the DIVI builder to add schema markup to your website using a builder you already know.

If you are in a competitive space or selling books and merchandise directly from your website, this can be important to your success.

Remember, your website is one of your most valuable assets, and SEO is a way to control how you rank and the attention your website receives.

Before discussing strategy, though, we will discuss common SEO pitfalls and how to avoid them. That's our next chapter.

FOURTEEN
AMAZON AS A SEARCH ENGINE

So far, we have been talking about SEO in terms of large, public search engines like Google and, to a lesser extent Bing and others. However, early on, we mentioned that Amazon and even your website can have a search engine.

And they work the same way Google does. They operate on keywords and algorithms just like Google and other search engines. In fact, right behind Google is YouTube (which parent company Alphabet owns) because people search for video content related to all kinds of things.

But when it comes to shopping, at least in the US, Amazon and Walmart top the list, and both are very good at what they do. This should interest you as an author primarily because the same type of keyword research you do to rank your website works to help you rank your books and author page on Amazon.

WHERE DO YOU PUT KEYWORDS ON AMAZON

The best way to think of Amazon and other retailers is as if your book page was a page on your website because it is just that, only on Amazon's website. They control some of the elements of the page, but you can control the text in your blurb and other areas, which makes for great SEO opportunities.

Things to think about include:

- Your metadata, the keywords you choose when you upload a new title
- Your book subtitle: you can include the genre or type of story here
- Your book blurb, including headings. Headings are different on Amazon and other book retailers, but they have the same effect as if they were on your website
- Your "from the publisher" and "editorial review" sections
- Your Amazon A+ Content

These areas almost deserve sections of their own to explain, but there are a lot of books out there that talk about how to set these up, what blurbs should look like, and more.

You can find a lot of information about these on the resources page on my website related to this book (you'll find it at the end of the book or in the companion course). For our purposes, we are going to focus on keywords.

How do you figure out what keywords you should aim for on Amazon?

MANUAL SEARCHES ON AMAZON

Just like manual keyword searches on other search engines, you can do the same thing on Amazon with one caveat: you can search logged out, but it is not the same as being entirely incognito. The technique works, but if you are signed into your personal account, recommendations will look different than if you are signed out.

Second, be sure when you do your searches that you do them in either the Kindle or Books section. With thousands of items on Amazon besides books in any given category, you might come up with some strange results that are not book related.

Use the same techniques as you would use on other search engines. Start typing keywords into the search bar and see what comes up. Just like with Google, you will get a list of keywords.

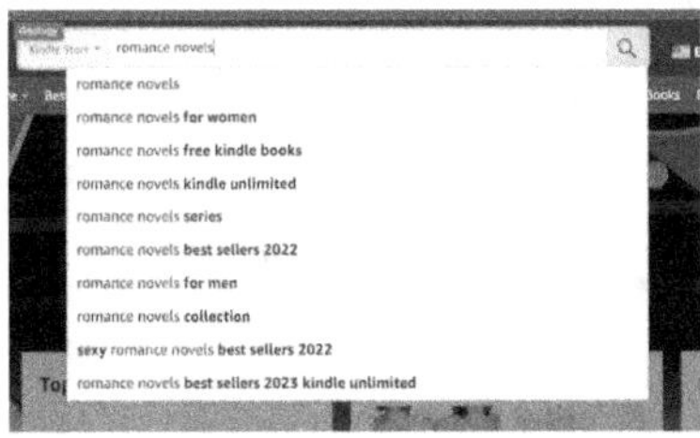

Those keywords will give you an idea of what people are searching for, and then you can do the same thing you did with Google: take the search terms related to your book and genre and enter them again, refining your search until you have a list you want.

Then compile your list and see how you can use them naturally in your book descriptions, headings, and text on Amazon and other retailers.

And just like with search engines, there are tools that can help you make your search faster and more thorough.

There are several tools, but I will spotlight a couple of the best and my favorites. Each does something unique, and each has its strengths. You can choose one or the other, but I'll show you how to use both here.

PUBLISHER ROCKET, KEYWORDS, AND CATEGORIES

Publisher Rocket, formerly KDP Rocket, is a research tool related to categories and keywords on Amazon. Keywords come in two types: search keywords and terms, which you should enter in your metadata when you upload and new title (and update from time to time), and AMS Keywords, which are keywords you would target with ads.

The two are very different, as Amazon has different rules for each. For instance, you cannot put "bestselling mystery fiction" in your metadata keywords, but you can target them with ads. The difference is the word "bestselling," which can be both objective and deceiving.

But the keywords you use in your metadata can also be used in your book descriptions, which translates to advertising. For example:

- A reader searches for "mystery books with dogs" on Amazon
- In your metadata for your book, which is a mystery that includes dogs, you have entered those two keywords (along with others) that signal Amazon what your book is about
- The reader finds your book. In your description, you say something about how dogs are involved in this mystery
- You have dogs in your A+ content and on your cover
- The reader finds that this is, indeed, a mystery with dogs, which is what they were searching for, and they hit "buy now"

This is how you align your books with your keywords and any ads you run. The reader could have clicked on an advertisement for your book if you rank near the top of that sub-search in Amazon or even a niche subcategory.

Categories are another topic, but if your category either contains or aligns with your keywords, that can also be a huge benefit.

Be careful with keyword lists, though, like the ones we got from AI or other tools: some will relate to your book better than others. The best ones align almost perfectly with your work. You also want readers who find your book to be satisfied after the purchase. While you might be able to rank in "romantic mysteries" with the right keywords and cover, if your book is not actually a romantic mystery, don't do this. In the long run, it will hurt you and your sales.

But there is another tool I like, and it works really well for diving into keywords and categories because it goes deeper than you can go with other tools. It's called K-Lytics.

K-LYTICS AND GENRE REPORTS

K-Lytics is a tool that offers in–depth genre reports complete with subgenres, niche categories, keywords, and trends. The most crucial difference between these tools is that K-Lytics gives a high-level overview of various markets, and KDP gives you a right-now snapshot (with few exceptions).

By looking at the trends in a specific subgenre or category, you can determine if a genre is on an upward trend, how it performs long term, and if it is a subgenre you can write and rank for. If it is, you can dive into titles, authors, and similar categories and use that information to figure out what you want to rank for.

K-Lytics does offer some free general market trend reports. These are both interesting and useful, but more valuable are the deep dive reports. These go in-depth into something specific, like female sleuths or cozy mysteries. You can look at the top covers over time, the top categories, subcategories, titles, subtitles, and more.

You'll almost know your book's chance of success before uploading it. The paid reports come out fairly often, so you can look at the latest information for your genre and category. It's extremely helpful.

OTHER TOOLS

There are other tools: KD-Spy and others, that work well also. You can also use more than one tool. My reports from K-Lytics give me data to research in Publisher Rocket, and that gives me categories that I can go back and study in more detail with K-Lytics. Other tools often work the same way.

The key is to find what tools work for you but to be aware of keywords and SEO while you craft your book blurb, subtitles, and more.

But remember, just like web content, your Book Blurb is only partly for Amazon's algorithms. It is also for readers who find your books and purchase them. The keywords must be inserted naturally. A title filled with keywords, which make no sense to readers, will never sell, at least not in the long run.

And publishing is a long game, as we know. Next, we'll look at common SEO mistakes and how to avoid them.

FIFTEEN

COMMON SEO PITFALLS (AND HOW TO AVOID THEM)

I n this chapter, we will discuss common SEO pitfalls to avoid to optimize your website effectively.

Black hat tactics are unethical or deceptive practices used to manipulate search engine rankings. These tactics can include spamming links, cloaking (showing different content to search engines than to users), and keyword stuffing (overusing keywords to manipulate rankings).

While these tactics may initially result in higher rankings, they can ultimately harm the credibility and authority of your website and lead to penalties from search engines. It's important to avoid black hat tactics and instead focus on building a solid website with high-quality content and genuine, earned links.

Let's look at what these are and how to avoid them.

CONTENT CLOAKING AND HOW TO AVOID DOING IT (EVEN ACCIDENTALLY)

Content cloaking is a black hat SEO technique that involves showing different content to search engines than what is offered to users. This can be done for various reasons, such as to manipulate search engine rankings or trick users into visiting a website. Content cloaking is generally considered a deceptive and unethical practice, and it is against the terms of service of most search engines, including Google.

Here are a few ways you can avoid content cloaking:

1. Don't show different content to search engines: The most effective way to prevent content cloaking is not to do it. Ensure that the content you show to search engines is the same as the content you show users.
2. Use a content delivery network (CDN): A CDN is a server network that delivers content to users based on their geographic location. By using a CDN, you can ensure that users worldwide see the same content, regardless of their location. Most web hosts include this as a part of their service. Just make sure yours is active and operating properly.
3. Use a responsive design: A responsive design ensures that your website automatically adjusts to fit the screen size and resolution of the device it's being viewed on. By using responsive design, you can ensure that all users see the same content, regardless of the device they are using.

Content cloaking is easy to avoid, and most people doing this are doing it on purpose. Just don't engage in it. For the most part, search engines find this quickly, which can result in a site being penalized or even delisted.

If you're puzzled about how this would even work, don't worry. It's not something you want or need to learn.

AVOID SPAMMY LINKS

Most often, spammy links are easy to avoid. First, don't buy links or guest posts on sites that are spammy in nature. For example, unless you write books on gambling or CBD, don't guest post on those sites to get backlinks. Most are filled with spam issues. Don't ever link to your site from a porn site, even if you write erotic fiction and it "fits your genre."

And if you do get a link from a spammy site, contact the site owner to have them either 'no-index' the link or remove it. If all else fails, disavow spammy links as a last resort.

It used to be standard practice for website owners to list their competition on spammy sites deliberately to get them into trouble and reduce their web authority. Not only is this poor and dishonest practice, but it is also illegal and easy to detect with modern tools. It's like negative review bombing, a common writer practice long ago. This is an attempt to increase your ranking by lowering someone else's.

First, this does not work. In fact, you will likely get caught, and instead of your competition being penalized, your site can be. This can include everything from reducing your rankings to delisting your site altogether.

 First, don't do this. Second, if you believe you are a victim of this kind of action, contact Google or other search engines directly. This is another reason to look at your link profile often and check your backlinks. In most cases, the search engine will help you resolve this quickly.

But if you must, work with an SEO pro to disavow links and restore your online reputation. And avoid deliberately getting spammy links no matter what the website owner promises you or how they try to reassure you. It will never end well.

AVOIDING KEYWORD STUFFING

Keyword stuffing is a black hat SEO technique that involves cramming as many keywords as possible into a webpage in an attempt to manipulate search engine rankings. This can be done in various ways, such as repeating the same keyword or using hidden text or links containing keywords.

Remember the guy we talked about who did this with a Superbowl article to outrank the actual website? He succeeded, but that success was temporary and costly. Hidden text and keywords are also equally problematic. Just avoid using them at all.

No matter the method, keyword stuffing is generally considered a deceptive and unethical practice, and it is against the terms of service of most search engines, including Google.

Here are a few ways you can avoid keyword stuffing:

1. Use keywords naturally: The best way to avoid keyword stuffing is to use keywords naturally in your content. Focus on creating high-quality, relevant content that naturally uses keywords and flows well.
2. Don't repeat keywords excessively: Using a keyword multiple times in your content is okay, but don't repeat it unnecessarily. Use keyword variations and mix them up with synonyms and related phrases to avoid keyword stuffing.
3. Use hidden text or links sparingly: If you need to use them on your website, use them as little as possible and only for legitimate purposes. Please don't use them to stuff keywords or manipulate search engine rankings in any other way.

Using an SEO tool like Yoast on your website can help, as it will flag words that are repeated too often and will offer warnings if you are engaged, even accidentally, in poor SEO practices.

Avoid keyword stuffing and ensure your website's content is high-quality and relevant. It's essential to focus on creating valuable, applicable content rather than trying to manipulate search engine rankings through deceptive techniques. That is what this book has been about, and if you follow the guidelines offered here, you'll avoid the risks of poor behavior.

AVOIDING GETTING DELISTED

There are several reasons why Google might delist (remove) a website from its search results. Here are a few examples:

1. Spam or manipulative tactics: Google takes a strict stance against spam and manipulative tactics and will delist websites that use these techniques. Examples of spam or manipulative tactics include the ones mentioned in this section, including keyword stuffing, cloaking, and using hidden text or links.
2. Malware or security issues: If a website is infected with malware or has security vulnerabilities, Google may delist it to protect users.
3. Violation of Google's webmaster guidelines: Google has a set of webmaster guidelines that outline the rules and best practices for building and maintaining a website. If a website violates these guidelines, it may be delisted.
4. Lack of original content: Google values original and high-quality content and may delist websites that do not have enough original content or that scrape content from other websites.
5. Lack of mobile-friendliness: With the increasing use of mobile devices to access the web, Google prefers mobile-

friendly websites in its search results. If a website is not mobile-friendly, it may be delisted.

If your website has been delisted, you can try to identify the reason and take steps to fix the issue, but being reinstated can be a long and complex process, so it is best to avoid it if possible.

WHAT TO DO IF YOUR SITE IS DELISTED

If you find yourself in the unfortunate position where Google has delisted your website, there are a few steps you can take to try to get it reinstated:

1. The first step is to try to determine why your website was delisted. Google provides information about the most common reasons for delisting in its webmaster guidelines, and you can also check the Google Search Console for any messages or warnings from Google about issues with your website.
2. Once you have identified the reason for the delisting, take steps to fix the issue. This might involve cleaning up spam or manipulative tactics, fixing malware or security vulnerabilities, or updating your website to meet Google's webmaster guidelines. You may need to bring in SEO, webmaster, or security pros to help you. Do it. It is worth it to be reinstated.
3. Once you have fixed the issue, you can request a review of your website through the Google Search Console. If the problem has been resolved, Google will review your website and may reinstate it in its search results.
4. After your website has been reinstated, it's important to continue monitoring it and following best practices to avoid future delistings. This includes avoiding spam or manipulative tactics, keeping your website secure and up-to-date, and providing high-quality, original content.

If you are delisted more than once, it is challenging to get reinstated, which may mean starting your website over from scratch with a new domain name and no ranking at all. The best cure is to prevent this from happening in the first place.

Common Mistakes Authors Make with SEO

While we have looked at general guidelines, we are focused on authors in this book. Here are a few common mistakes that authors make when optimizing their websites:

1. Not conducting keyword research: Failing to identify relevant keywords can result in targeting the wrong terms and not reaching the right audience.
2. Not optimizing for mobile: As mentioned previously, ensuring your website is optimized for mobile to reach a wider audience and improve your rankings is essential.
3. Ignoring the user experience: It's important to provide a positive user experience to keep visitors on your website and encourage them to take desired actions (such as purchasing a book).
4. Not regularly updating content: Search engines favor websites with fresh, relevant content. It's important to periodically update your website with new content both for the algorithm and to keep visitors coming back

Writers tend to go through spurts of "I should fix my website" or "I should blog more," followed by periods of inactivity while they write that next novel or between releases when they feel like they "have nothing to say." (Ask me how I know this).

This is a colossal error. If you must, hire someone to help you keep your site current. Work with other authors and hold each other accountable. Your SEO will suffer, as will your rankings, and when you need them to be the best they can be, you'll be working to rebuild and bring them back up.

Neglect kills websites and SEO quicker than anything. Want to avoid it? Update your site regularly and do frequent checks to make sure everything is still working. Look at your rankings often for vital keywords, and if you start slipping down the ranks, look at why and what you can do about it.

Next, we'll look at one final thing: creating an overall SEO Strategy.

SIXTEEN
DEVELOPING YOUR OWN SEO STRATEGY

As we have discussed, developing an effective SEO strategy is essential for authors to increase their online visibility and attract a larger audience. Developing an SEO strategy for yourself involves taking each element of this book, applying it to your own website books, and integrating it with your marketing strategy.

We've talked about all of these, but now it is time to pull them all together.

KEYWORD RESEARCH:

Conduct thorough keyword research to identify the most relevant and high-traffic keywords related to your book genre, topics, and target audience. We discussed tools like Google Keyword Planner, SEMrush, or MOZ, and even AI like ChatGPT that can help you find valuable keywords.

But it is time to build your own list. You can even use book tools like Publisher Rocket that analyze Amazon keywords and then plug them into your overall keyword strategy.

Remember to update this keyword list often. Whenever you write or release a new book, add a bit of another genre, or Amazon changes its algorithm, take another look at your keywords. Then center your content, book descriptions, and all your efforts around those keywords.

A note: these keywords can also help you discover keywords and categories on Amazon and other retailers and even inform your marketing keywords for ads on Facebook and BookBub.

Keywords are the core of your SEO and your marketing strategy. Start here, and get this right, and the rest of your SEO efforts will be much easier.

OPTIMIZED WEBSITE:

Create and maintain an author website that is optimized for both search engines and users. Ensure your website is mobile-friendly, loads quickly, and provides a positive user experience. Organize your content logically and create individual pages for each book, complete with compelling book descriptions, reviews, and purchase links. Integrate your keywords everywhere, including metadata, titles, and even through more advanced schema markup and structured data.

The two things you have the most control and ownership over are your email subscribers and your website. Maximize the quality of each, and you'll be less dependent on social media and third-party platforms.

Your keywords and setting up your website properly are the first two and most vital steps in your SEO strategy.

META TAGS AND DESCRIPTIONS:

Pay attention to your website's meta tags, including meta titles and meta descriptions. Use relevant keywords in these tags to help search engines understand the content of your pages and posts.

Well-optimized meta tags can improve click-through rates from search engine results pages (SERPs) because you rank higher for relevant topics. This runs through everything you will do, from content creation to page creation and more.

QUALITY CONTENT CREATION:

Produce high-quality and engaging content related to your books and writing niche. Regularly publish blog posts, articles, or guest posts that incorporate your target keywords and provide value to your readers. Fresh and informative content will help attract organic traffic and establish you as an authority in your field.

Also, show that you are in touch with what is happening in your genre, from other books to entertainment like movies and television series. Your content should establish that you are an expert: from relationships (as a romance writer) to law enforcement and forensic techniques (like mystery authors) to a period of history or occupation.

You are, and should be, the world's leading expert on your book and what it is about. It's an opportunity that puts you potentially in the spotlight. Please don't neglect this, but instead embrace it.

BACKLINK BUILDING:

Once you have good content to link to that establishes you as an expert, focus on acquiring high-quality backlinks to your website from reputable and relevant sources. Guest posting on other author or even industry blogs, collaborating with book reviewers, and participating in interviews or podcast features can help you build a strong backlink profile, a crucial factor in SEO.

There are all kinds of ways to build backlinks. The more in touch you are in your genre, and the more you are seen as an expert, the more opportunity you will have. Offer to write columns, features, guest posts, and more. Focus on quality, although quantity matters too.

Blog tours, podcast tours, and other opportunities help you build your brand and reputation while improving your SEO. Remember, SEO takes time. Just keep at it, and you'll get better as you go.

SOCIAL MEDIA PROMOTION:

Leverage social media platforms to engage with your audience and promote your content. Share your blog posts, book updates, and other content on platforms like Twitter, Facebook, Instagram, and LinkedIn. Social signals can indirectly impact your search engine rankings.

GOOGLE MY BUSINESS (GMB) PROFILE:

For local SEO benefits, claim and optimize your Google My Business profile. Fill in accurate and up-to-date information, such as your address, phone number, and business hours. This will help Google display your information in local searches.

Remember, you don't have to use your address if you do not have an office outside your home. But this can earn you readers and customers. I know authors who have received more than 200 profile views and several contacts monthly. For those who also offer author services, that can be even higher.

This seems silly and even an extra step to many authors, but it can be worthwhile over time. Also, it can increase your Google rankings and improve SEO overall, even if you don't get local referrals or readers as a result.

OPTIMIZED BOOK TITLES AND DESCRIPTIONS:

Optimize your book titles and descriptions on online retailers like Amazon or Barnes & Noble. Use keywords that potential readers are likely to search for when looking for books in your genre. A well-crafted book description can also entice readers to click and make a purchase.

As we mentioned in this book, this also ties into your overall SEO. Those keywords impact your website, your advertising, and more. Search your title, and make sure it is not taken by another author in your genre. Consider your subtitle as another keyword opportunity. Include keywords in your book description when possible.

Remember to do this naturally and not force it. Don't overuse keywords and stuff them, either. Remember, Amazon is also a search engine, and your book page is a webpage. Optimize it like you would a page on your own site.

And speaking of your own site, you should have a page for each book and series with many keywords similar to your Amazon pages. This is especially true if you are going to sell books directly to readers.

REGULAR WEBSITE AUDITS AND MAINTENANCE:

Periodically review your website's performance and conduct SEO audits to identify areas for improvement. Check for broken links, update outdated content, and ensure your website is aligned with the latest SEO best practices. Look, this is probably best done monthly or at least once a quarter. You want to see how your site is doing and if it needs improvement or even repair.

Use the tools we talked about in this book, but also look at your pages and blog posts. Check titles, SEO scores, and more to ensure your site operates smoothly. Use Google tools to ensure your site speed is still adequate, and look at it on different devices to ensure it is responsive and fast.

Your website health is like your personal health. It's important to check regularly to make sure it is healthy.

MONITOR AND ANALYZE PERFORMANCE:

Utilize tools like Google Analytics and Search Console to monitor the performance of your website and track essential metrics such as organic traffic, keyword rankings, and user behavior. Analyzing these metrics will help you refine your SEO strategy over time.

Look at what pages perform best and what keywords you rank for. Check out bounce rates, referral and social traffic, and other data to ensure your site works how you want and need it to.

Remember that SEO is an ongoing process that may take time to see significant results. Consistency, quality content, and staying up to date with SEO trends are key to a successful SEO strategy for authors, just like for other businesses.

All these steps are important, and missing one or more can result in your site dropping in ranking and activity, directly impacting your income and livelihood as an author. But still, keep in mind that the best thing you can do as a writer is write. Set up your website, consider SEO, monitor, test, and all the rest. But SEO is not your job. Writing is, so be sure to schedule and dedicate time to your website outside of your writing time.

And if it gets too complex and you need help or just to save time? Hire a pro. Sometimes that's the best investment you can make.

You're almost there. I've brought you through most of what you need to know about SEO and pointed you to resources about the rest. But what now?

SEVENTEEN
CONCLUSION AND NEXT STEPS

Congratulations on finishing this book! Now what?
First, let's review some key takeaways:

- SEO is the practice of optimizing a website to improve its visibility and ranking in search engine results pages (SERPs).
- Keyword research is essential for identifying the most relevant keywords to target on your website.
- On-page optimization involves optimizing a web page's content and HTML source code to improve its ranking in search results.
- Off-page optimization involves activities that take place outside of your website, such as building links and generating social media shares, to improve its visibility and authority.
- It's important to track and analyze your website's performance using key performance indicators (KPIs) to identify areas for improvement.

- Advanced SEO techniques, such as local SEO and schema markup, can help take your optimization efforts to the next level.
- Avoiding common SEO pitfalls, such as black hat tactics and ignoring the user experience, is crucial for building a strong, credible website.

That's about as high level as we can go. We've covered each of those sections in detail, and there are all kinds of tools and resources we have talked about that are related. I recommend that you come back and review this material often. Keep up with SEO trends and adapt as needed. However, no matter what is next, these principles are foundational and stay close to the same over time.

So, what do you do once your site is up and running? Here are some next steps:

- Continue to conduct keyword research and update your website's content with relevant, high-quality content. Be consistent, above all.
- Focus on building high-quality, relevant links to your website. Remember, this is another area where consistency pays.
- Regularly track and analyze your website's performance using tools such as Google Analytics, MOZ, SEMrush, or SEOCrawl.
- Consider implementing advanced SEO techniques, such as local SEO or schema markup, to improve your website's visibility and credibility further.
- Stay up to date with the latest SEO trends and best practices to continually improve your website's SEO.

And that's it. There are many free resources on my website related to this book, and you can always reach out for a consultation if you need help. But with that, go forth and do wonderful SEO things.

I know you'll have the success you deserve if you put in the work. It's true for any part of your author career, including SEO.

ABOUT THE AUTHOR

Troy Lambert is a full-time writer and author. Having written over thirty mysteries and other novels, Troy is well-versed in story creation, and he knows what it takes to make a fictional story real! Troy's hobbies and pastimes (when he's able to break away from the computer) include hiking into the mountains of Southwest Idaho, fishing in a fast-rushing stream, and going for a drive where his mind can work on creating that perfect twist to the book he's currently writing. A native of Idaho Falls, Idaho, Troy lives in the mountains of Idaho. You can find his other works, including his latest book, *Teaching Moments*, at troylambertwrites.com.

ALSO BY TROY LAMBERT

THE MAX BOUCHER SERIES:

Teaching Moments

Harvested

THE SAMUEL ELIJAH JOHNSON SERIES

Redemption

Temptation

Confession

MONSTER MARSHALS

Miner Inconveniences

Tilting at Windmills

NON-FICTION

The Tao of Trek

Writing as a Business: Production, Distribution, and Marketing

The Pocket Guide to Plotting

THE DOG COMPLEX

Stray Ally